WAKE UP
OR
BREAK UP

WAKE UP

8 CRUCIAL STEPS
TO STRENGTHENING YOUR RELATIONSHIP

OR

LEONARD FELDER, PH.D.
COAUTHOR OF MAKING PEACE WITH YOUR PARENTS

BREAK UP

Printed in the United States of America
Rodale Inc. makes every effort to use acid-free ∞, recycled paper ♻.

Book design by Tara Long

Library of Congress Cataloging-in-Publication Data

Felder, Leonard.
    Wake up or break up : 8 crucial steps to strengthening your relationship / Leonard Felder.
       p.   cm.
    Includes bibliographical references.
    ISBN-13 978–1–59486–072–0 hardcover
    ISBN-10 1–59486–072–6 hardcover
    1. Marriage.   2. Man-woman relationships.   3. Couples.   I. Title.
HQ734.F3715   2005
646.7'8—dc22   2005000380

Distributed to the trade by Holtzbrinck Publishers

2   4   6   8   10   9   7   5   3   1   hardcover

We inspire and enable people to improve their lives and the world around them
For more of our products visit **rodalestore.com** or call 800-848-4735

To my wife, Linda Schorin,
who has been my partner,
best friend, creative adventurer,
and lover for more than twenty-four years,
and who amazes me often
with her honesty, her courage,
and her love of life

.

CONTENTS

INTRODUCTION: A Moment of Clarity   3

STEP ONE: Striking a Balance between Being
Too Flexible and Not Flexible Enough   9

STEP TWO: Making Your Intimate Moments
More Satisfying   43

STEP THREE: Navigating the Daily Transition
from Work Mode to Fully Present   87

STEP FOUR: Making Domestic Teamwork More
"Team" and Less "Work"   111

STEP FIVE: Resolving Frustrations
Before They Get Ugly   131

STEP SIX: Dealing with Challenging
People Who Are Part of the Package   153

STEP SEVEN: Coming Through for Each
Other during Life's Tough Moments   181

STEP EIGHT: Keeping Your Relationship
Strong Year after Year   209

ACKNOWLEDGMENTS   237

NOTES AND SOURCES   239

partner will begin to approach every important conversation as true partners.

A feeling of frustration or disappointment regarding your sex life. If one or both of you are unhappy with the frequency or quality of your intimacy, there are some highly enjoyable remedies to help prevent affairs or bitter resentments that may tear apart your relationship. Specifically, in chapters 2, 6, and 8, you will learn thoughtful actions to improve the quality of your intimate moments together and bring passion, sensuality, and closeness back into your relationship—even if the two of you are frequently stressed, tired, or deeply skeptical about the possibility of a revived sexuality.

A feeling that certain people or situations are driving a wedge between you. If you and your partner have been upset with each other because of work pressures, relatives, kids, exes, or other de-manding people or situations, there are some effective and creative ways to resolve these issues. In chapters 1, 3, 7, and especially chapter 6, you will be given easy-to-utilize methods for building a stronger and more united front with your partner, no matter who or what tries to split you up. Rather than being at the mercy of these outside forces, the two of you should know exactly how to be strong allies no matter what crises or challenges arise.

A feeling of exasperation because your clashes are too frequent or too hurtful. When two strong-minded or strong-willed people get together, there are bound to be differences of opinion and oc-casional disputes. Especially if one of you has a quick temper, a tendency to shut down emotionally, or a habit of saying hurtful or provocative things during a fight, you will be pleased to learn about a successful technique for resolving clashes more quickly and with less strife. In chapters 5 and 7, I share a proven method for cooling down and for regaining your ability to work as true partners who see things differently but who benefit from combining unique points of view.

By restoring the teamwork, intimacy, and mutual respect that have been lacking lately because of the pressures and stresses, you will be giving your relationship the much-needed tune-up that you or your partner senses it requires.

IT WILL GET BETTER

As you read about the eight steps I lay out in this book, you'll see that I don't waste time with vague theories or fancy academic terminology. Instead, each step includes a practical set of tools with vivid real-life examples for doing what works and avoiding what doesn't. For twenty years I've been testing these methods with more than a thousand couples from a variety of backgrounds—married couples, unmarried couples, heterosexuals, gays, lesbians, childless couples, couples with young kids, couples with grown children—all of whom came in for counseling or attended one of my one-day workshops. I've found that in almost 80 percent of cases these methods work to dramatically strengthen and improve even the most shaky relationships—not only in the short run but for years afterward. According to surveys, that 80 percent success rate is much better than for traditional couples counseling or for self-help books. The key difference is that each of these eight techniques was developed by the couples, rather than by the therapist. They taught me (as their therapist) exactly what made things better in their relationship, versus what seemed like a good idea in theory but didn't work as effectively in real life.

These eight short chapters spell out one at a time the crucial steps and most effective solutions for transforming your love life from one of frustration into one of shared satisfaction. You and your partner might not need to read all eight chapters. Look at the table of contents to decide which steps offer the solutions that will quickly improve your particular relationship. Then, later on, when your current crisis has subsided, you can explore the additional relationship-enhancing methods in the other chapters. My sincere hope is that one or more of these eight steps will help you experience the moments of trust, warmth, teamwork, and passion that you've been missing.

Please do yourself and your partner a favor: Instead of passively waiting for some catastrophe to devastate your relationship, start right now using the steps in this book to dramatically improve your potentially wonderful partnership.

STRIKING A BALANCE BETWEEN BEING TOO FLEXIBLE AND NOT FLEXIBLE ENOUGH

It's bigger than sex. Tougher than even the most difficult relative. And able to wreak havoc among unsuspecting couples, no matter how committed they are. Welcome to the number one issue that can make or break up your long-term relationship: flexibility.

I've found that flexibility toward and accommodation of your partner's way of doing things is crucial for almost every relationship. No matter how much you love each other or want things to go smoothly, in any given week the issue of flexibility versus inflexibility is likely to pop up. Several years ago, the actress and novelist Carrie Fisher (who played Princess Leia in *Star Wars* and later wrote *Postcards from the Edge* and other books) described this exhausting power struggle quite vividly when explaining her breakup from musician Paul Simon. "In many relationships one person gets to be the flower while the other person tends to be the one who waters, nurtures, and supports the flower," she said. "In our relationship we kept fighting over who gets to be the flower and neither of us wanted to be the one who nurtures the flower."

Numerous research studies show that one of the clearest early indications of a good relationship starting to go downhill is one partner feeling he or she is giving in too often and not being respected or taken seriously. For example, in the research studies of Dr. John Gottman at the University of Washington, the most satisfied couples were those who felt their generosity and goodwill were being reciprocated; when one or both partners felt slighted, let down, or taken for granted, there was lots of tension. I've found in hundreds of cases in my own practice that the most successful way to move your relationship out of danger is for you and your partner to learn specific skills and strategies for bringing more balance and fairness to each decision and interaction with each other.

To see if there is an imbalance upsetting your own relationship, answer the following questions honestly.

* Do you ever feel as if you're being too accommodating to your partner?
* Have you been putting your own needs on hold lately?
* Has your partner ever criticized you for not being assertive enough with a difficult member of your extended family, a co-worker who drains you constantly, a waiter, a hotel clerk, or some other person who wasn't doing a good job?
* Do you sometimes go out of your way to do nice things for someone you love in the hope that he or she will reciprocate, but instead this person seems to take you for granted?
* Do you ever have trouble admitting what you want in lovemaking, in structuring your weekends, or in making plans for the future?

✳ Do you spend so much energy responding to the crises of daily life that sometimes when your partner asks you for one more thing it pushes you to the breaking point?

If you answered yes to two or more of these questions, you probably have a tendency to be too flexible. On the other hand,

✳ Have you ever been told by your current or former partner that you are selfish, stubborn, demanding, or unavailable?

✳ Have you ever been accused of being rigid, bossy, or controlling, even when you think you're just expressing your point of view?

✳ Do you ever find sneaky ways to get your needs met without letting your partner know?

✳ Has your partner ever accused you of being too loud, rude, or argumentative with someone you confronted at a dinner party, a social event, or your kid's school event, or with someone who works in a service capacity?

✳ Do you ever lash out in anger or sarcasm because you feel your partner isn't as orderly, neat, or punctual as you?

✳ Do you ever feel so sure of what you believe that you honestly don't want to hear your loved one's differing point of view?

If you answered yes to at least two of the questions above, then you probably are somewhat rigid at times. In either case—whether you or your partner are too flexible or not flexible enough—a simple adjustment in attitude could restore balance and harmony to your relationship.

BOTH OF YOU CAN GET MORE OF WHAT YOU WANT

A woman named Katrina came into my office with her husband Jack one morning a few months ago and opened the session by saying, "First and foremost, I want you to know that I do love my husband. Jack is a good person. Really, he's done a lot of wonderful things for many people. But sometimes he can be so stubborn. I know it's a part of who he is and I'm supposed to love him unconditionally and all that hoo-hah. But there are times when his selfish, controlling side rears its ugly head and I feel like I'm gonna scream. He doesn't do it all the time, but when Jack gets that rigid, I've-got-to-have-it-my-way, end-of-discussion look in his eyes, it's such a complete turn-off."

What made Katrina's comments especially interesting is that an hour later a woman named Paula came into my office with her husband, Allen, and said, "I love my husband. Really, I do. I just wish sometimes Allen could be a little more assertive or articulate about what he wants and needs. I think he is way too much of a people-pleaser and, as a result, you never know if he's doing something because he wants to or because he feels he has to. I appreciate that Allen is caring and kind by nature, but there are times when I need him to have a little more backbone—to speak up and stand a little stronger so I don't have to feel like I'm married to a pushover."

Later that same day, a film director named Amy showed up in my office with her partner of seven years, a highly respected middle-school guidance counselor named Rebecca. According to

Amy, "I know Rebecca has a good heart and that she means well. But she spends so much energy and time taking care of her troubled students, her aging mom, and her impossible younger sister that she's got almost nothing left over for me or our relationship. Every night she's on the phone, handling one crisis or another, so that whenever I ask for something from her, or for her to consider my needs and be flexible once in a while, it's as though I'm asking for too much. Rebecca even admitted recently that she's burned out from trying so hard to help everyone else and so she doesn't have much left over to give me. On one level I understand she's overloaded, but there's a part of me that asks, 'What am I, chopped liver?'"

These three couples with essentially decent relationships are dealing with the same painful frustration: how to strike a balance between being too flexible and not flexible enough.

The proven techniques and suggestions described in this chapter are designed to make sure you and your partner *both* get the nurturing you want and need in your relationship. They will help you prevent arguments and hurt feelings that may eat away at your relationship, and they will help you build bonds to bring you closer. If you tend to be the "my way is the right way" person, my goal is to help you lighten up a bit and be more giving, without ignoring your own desires and feelings. If you are a bit too accommodating or selfless, I'll help you find clear and appropriate ways to express your equally valid needs and insights so that the relationship becomes more balanced.

THE FOUR IMBALANCERS

Four kinds of personalities may throw off the balance of a relationship. Sometimes a partner will fit one description to a T. Other times, a partner will exhibit the characteristics of one trait just a bit but even this small amount sometimes disrupts the relationship. Remember, our goal is to achieve a *balance* between partners, where each is flexible enough to respect the other's desires without becoming a doormat.

As you read over the following descriptions of the causes of imbalance between assertiveness and flexibility, please be honest with yourself. Are any of the habits similar to your behavior in your current or previous relationships? Or are they issues that you wish your partner would face up to and resolve so that the overall relationship could be a lot more satisfying for both of you?

THE UNINTENTIONAL BULLDOZER

Have you ever found out after an important discussion with your partner that he or she was feeling lectured or bullied by you? Have you ever been told by a loved one, "Don't yell at me," when you didn't think you were yelling? Have you been accused of being too rushed, too demanding, or so insistent that others can't get a word in edgewise when you simply were trying to make a point in a discussion about which you were passionate?

What's the deal here? Are these people overreacting, or is it possible that you might unintentionally be acting like a bulldozer?

I've found that the majority of "unintentional bulldozers" don't realize just how worked up and uncompromising they sound to other people. When it seems as if your partner doesn't understand your point of view or is contradicting you, it may cause you to speak a bit too loudly, or to say things dramatically or with a little too much finality. You may be just trying to make a logical, rational case, and yet the other person is hearing only how strongly you want to get your way. You may not really want to verbally squash your loved one, but like the character Lenny in John Steinbeck's *Of Mice and Men*, the passionate soul who longs for a beloved rabbit companion but then squeezes it too tightly, you might be more intense than you realize.

This doesn't make you a bad person. Many decent and caring men and women just can't hold back when they're agitated, upset, or very concerned about something that is being discussed. Ultimately, though, if your partner senses a rigidity or an inflexibility that shuts down important conversations, it will cause problems in your relationship.

BREAKING THE BULLDOZER HABIT

When your partner or one of your kids says, "You're yelling," or "You're not listening to me," your first reaction may be to feel defensive and to insist, "I'm not yelling! Don't tell me I'm yelling when I know I'm not yelling!"

Let's look at another, more successful response. When someone you love tells you that you're being a bit of a bulldozer, or if in mid-discussion you become aware of this yourself, I suggest taking a deep breath, opening up your heart, and calling on your sense of humor as you say to yourself, "If it sounds to my loved one like I'm being a bulldozer, and if it feels to my loved one like I'm being a bulldozer, then for the sake of being a great partner, let me think of myself, for a moment, as a bulldozer."

Rather than getting defensive or launching a verbal counterattack, take your partner's words to heart. This is no time for a debate about decibel levels, deeper intentions, or who got testy first. The best way to make progress right now is to quickly catch yourself and ask your partner—preferably with a bit of humor, charm, or irony in your voice—"Am I being a bit of a bulldozer right now?" That won't mean you're giving in or taking all the blame for the miscommunication between the two of you. It just means you are becoming a more conscious person. You are breaking an old habit so that you and your lover can respectfully negotiate. Admitting to yourself and your partner that, "Yep, I probably sounded a bit like a bulldozer right then" is going to feel like a breath of fresh air to the vulnerable human being who was starting to feel bullied or frustrated by your intense verbal style. It's like a declaration of peace in what could have become a long and nasty war.

Now take a deep breath and say gently the following words to dramatically change the quality of your interactions with these precious souls who need your calmness and patience. The magic words are: "Let me be quiet for a few moments and hear your take on the situation. I won't interrupt you. I do want to know your side of things."

16

I realize it might not be easy or automatic for you to talk like this, especially when your brain is saying, "But I'm 100 percent right and the other person is 100 percent wrong!" This is what your brain does when adrenaline is pumping and you are facing a challenge. You might be wondering, "Do I really have to be the big person here? Why do I have to be the one to make an offering of peace?" But if you can override the automatic responses of your brain and say just these few words during a heated discussion, I can almost guarantee you will be amazed by the results. Your sense of humor and your sense of teamwork are two of the most powerful tools you have for taking your relationship to a much higher level of trust and closeness.

"I Was Just Trying to Make a Point"

When I think of all the passionate and intelligent bulldozers I've met in my counseling practice, one particular guy named Chris comes to mind. Chris is a highly articulate attorney who almost always outsmarts opposing attorneys in the courtroom. He's got a quick mind, a strong sense of integrity, and a deep desire to win. So when he sits across from his soft-spoken wife, Julia, and they try to work out their differences, Chris naturally speaks in an intense and argumentative style.

One day in a couples-counseling session, Chris's in-your-face style brought Julia to tears, even though he insisted, "I was just trying to make a point." So I offered Chris the tool of catching himself and asking Julia, with a humorous tone, "Am I being a bit of a bulldozer right now?" That one sentence broke the tension between them and allowed Julia to begin to regain her strength so that they could negotiate as equals.

Then Chris said the magic words I had recommended as the second phrase: "Let me be quiet for a few minutes and hear your take on the situation. I won't interrupt, and I do want to know your side of things." As soon as Chris said those comforting words, you could see Julia relaxing and warming up to him. Even though it was not his usual way of responding, Chris was willing to break his old habit of being a bulldozer if it meant that he and Julia could start being loving partners again.

According to Julia, "All I need is for Chris to stop his argumentative style for one minute so I can catch my breath and not feel like I have to justify every word out of my mouth. I wish he could admit sometimes that he's a bit intimidating when he's really worked up about something. He's not mean or intentionally hurtful; he's just very intense and passionate. If he can show me those few moments of calmness or patience, I know we can come up with workable solutions to whatever we're discussing and be on a much more equal footing. I know in my heart that Chris wants me to be his equal when we have these discussions, but sometimes I need him to stop and catch himself for a moment so I can regain my strength and not feel so drained by his intense style."

"She Talks to Me Like I'm a Child or an Employee"

Another example of how we sometimes act like an unintentional bulldozer is the case of Patrice and Donna. They've been together for three years and recently purchased a first home where they are raising Donna's two kids from a previous relationship. To outsiders, they look like a great couple.

But Donna explains, "Patrice is an extremely competent and organized person at her job. The trouble is, when she comes home from work, she talks to me like I'm a child or an employee. I don't think she intends to be condescending or hurtful, but there's something disrespectful in the way she talks to me when the kids are acting up or the house is messy. Patrice gets an intense look on her face and she lectures me like I'm somehow at fault."

It took several weeks in counseling for Patrice and Donna to develop a more respectful and less agitating way of giving each other feedback and suggestions about child-care and housework issues. The breakthrough for Patrice came when she began using the technique described above. Instead of continuing to bombard Donna with boss-like questions about why the house wasn't spotless or why the kids were misbehaving, Patrice would catch herself, take a deep breath, open up her heart, and say, "Am I being a bit of a bulldozer right now?" Then Patrice would calmly and lovingly say, "Let me be quiet for a few minutes and hear your take on the situation. I won't interrupt, and I do want to know your side of things."

As Donna commented during their final counseling session, "I always knew in my gut that Patrice wasn't an arrogant or hurtful person. So in the past when she would talk to me like I was one-down from her, it always felt strange. I'm glad she was willing to see a counselor and work on this before it got to the point where I resented her and wanted to end our relationship. The kids still act up sometimes and the house isn't perfectly neat all the time, but now there's something noticeably different about the way Patrice discusses these issues with me. There's a definite caring and a sense of mutual respect that was missing from her tone of voice for quite a while, but now it's almost always there so we can be teammates again and not get on each other's nerves half as often."

No one likes to be talked to in a demeaning way. If you or your partner talk to each other at times in a harsh, patronizing, or controlling tone of voice, please take a positive step as soon as possible to remove this thorn from your relationship. Either on your own or with a counselor, make a serious effort to bury your bulldozer ways—or the one you're bulldozing just might rise up one day and walk out the door.

THE MARTYR

At the opposite end of the assertiveness spectrum from the bulldozer is the man or woman who has trouble speaking up in a direct manner and admitting his or her needs honestly: the whiner, or martyr. Whining and acting like a victim to generate sympathy, make your partner feel guilty, or get your way is quite common, even among very powerful and successful men and women who can speak up just fine in a work setting but are tongue-tied guilt trippers in their personal lives.

A whiner is likely to have an arsenal of stock phrases intended to make his or her partner feel guilty, such as "But you promised," "You never let me," "You're so selfish," "You always want things your way," or the ever-popular, "Well, your friend Susan never has a problem with that. . . ." Or the whiner will sulk with a sad face that implies, "I'm in terrible emotional pain right now and it's completely your fault." Some people even become whiners and martyrs in the bedroom, trying to convince a reluctant partner to have sex by saying, "But you promised" or "If we don't do it soon, I'm going to explode" or "Yo, I'm dyin' here." I remember one of my counseling clients, a top executive named Justin, who was able to find humor in his own occasional habit of whining. He said, "If only whining was a turn-on for my partner, we'd be having a lot more sex than we do."

Sometimes whining and guilt trips do work for a while. But let's be honest: Most of us don't enjoy being manipulated or guilt-tripped. That tack might generate a few half-hearted surrenders in the short run, but after a few months or years it usually leads to the other partner losing respect or affection for the adult who plays the child-like victim.

If you find that you have resorted to whining in order to get what you want in your relationship, stop this unappealing strategy before it causes your partner to clam up permanently. Or, if your partner is the one who sometimes lays a guilt trip with a puppy dog expression, you both can break the habit with the following method, a playful and extremely effective technique that I've used successfully with many couples.

21

LIGHTEN UP!

This method almost always works when a whining tone of voice or a sulking look starts to emerge. Catch yourself instantly and, with a bit of humor, say to yourself or your partner, "Whoa, watch out, whiner alert!" or something similarly silly. You and your partner can create your own humorous phrase, as long as it is something that helps you stop the whining impulse before it builds a permanent wall between you.

After you catch yourself, ask your partner in a direct and adult way for the things you previously would have whined about. The easiest way to do this is simply to say calmly and respectfully, "There's something I want to request" or "There's something I want us to consider." You might get a yes or a no in response—that part isn't within your control. What you can control is whether you talk to your partner as one self-respecting adult to another. If you feel shy or insecure around your partner, you might want to consider counseling to help strengthen your ability to speak up. Some people with a lifelong history of social phobia or chronic shyness have been helped enormously by individual therapy, support groups, assertiveness courses, or even medication. You may want to consult a qualified professional to figure out which course of action might be right for you.

If your shyness is less severe, you might try saying a few honest and inspiring things to yourself right at the moment when you are tempted to revert to whining or silent martyrdom. You might say to yourself, "My partner cares about me and, whether I receive a yes or a no to this particular request, I know my partner wants to hear what I need." Or you might say to yourself, "Even a caring and gentle no from my beloved is better than silence or distance between us. And who knows? I might actually get a yes!"

"Guilt Trips Used to Work Pretty Well for Me"

A few months ago I counseled a couple in which the husband, Dennis, was a decisive and competent engineer at work but a whiner at home with his wife. Dennis often tried to get Elaine to back down and let him win arguments or let him have his way on important decisions by whining, sulking, and acting like a martyr. For years she had put up with his guilt trips, but more recently she had begun to shut down toward him emotionally. It didn't surprise me to hear that their sex life had become a distant memory.

In our counseling sessions we explored why Dennis was such a competent adult at work but had become a whiner around the people he cared about the most. Sadly, he had grown up with two very self-involved parents who never took his needs seriously. No matter what Dennis said or how he asked, his parents were usually too busy or too self-absorbed to listen carefully and respond appropriately to what he was requesting. So Dennis had decided that being direct didn't work, and, as a result, he tended to hide or disguise his needs.

At first this approach was more or less successful for Dennis. "Guilt trips used to work pretty well for me," he said during a counseling session. "With my ex-wife, I could get her to compromise and give me what I wanted if I made her see how unhappy she was making me. All I had to say was, 'You're being selfish' or 'You promised,' and at least half the time she would feel guilty and back down. That is, until she eventually had an affair and left the marriage."

Dennis continued, "Early in my relationship with Elaine, the same tactics worked quite well. I would get a hurt and sad look on my face and I might say something like, 'But don't you care how I feel?' or 'How could you be so selfish?' and Elaine would usually feel horrible and let me have my way. Then, after a few years, I noticed the guilt trips no longer worked so well. Instead of feeling guilty and backing down, Elaine just became more angry and distant."

Over the next several weeks, Dennis began to catch himself whenever he was tempted to do the whiner/martyr thing. He would sometimes remind himself silently, "I'm an adult. I'm a very competent engineer, and I don't need to be a whiner with my wife." Or if a whiny or guilt-inducing phrase slipped out of his mouth, he would catch himself and quickly say out loud to Elaine, in a humorous tone of voice, "Was that the Whiners calling again? Tell them we're not home."

The two of them would laugh for a moment and then Elaine would ask, "Is there something you'd like? I'm not promising you're gonna get exactly what you ask for, but I do care about you, and if you ask like a grown-up instead of a whiner, your chances are a helluva lot better." Then Dennis would take a deep breath and ask Elaine in a direct and calm way for what he wanted.

This technique was the beginning of a breakthrough for them because the more Dennis acted like a competent adult around

Elaine, the more she regained her affection for him. Pretty soon they even revived their long-dormant love life. With a bit of playfulness in her voice, Elaine made a new rule for their lovemaking: "Any guilt trips or whining in the bedroom and you get to sleep down the hall. But if you approach me like a lover who will survive whether I say yes or no, then more often than not, it's gonna be yes."

As with many couples I have counseled, Elaine and Dennis were a lot happier with each other once they asked the Whiners to leave. If the Whiners are still a frequent or occasional visitor in your own relationship, I hope you will try out some of the same tools to help them make an exit.

THE UNILATERAL DECISION-MAKER

Now we come to a third tricky behavior that disrupts the balance of a relationship and creates substantial friction between partners. When you have to make a major decision about your career, vacation plans, weekend plans, or the purchase of a home, a car, or something less expensive for around the house—a sofa, lamp, barbecue grill, lawn ornament, video equipment, sound system, or other item—do you automatically consult with your partner about the best choice for both of you? Or do you sometimes listen to the part of your brain that is saying, "Naaaaah, I don't need to run this by anyone. It would be a lot easier and less complicated if I just made the decision on my own and told my partner there was no time for consultation."

Even couples who love each other a lot and who strongly value fairness and good communication may make hasty or one-sided decisions without taking seriously the other person's point of view. There seems to be a basic human urge for control that even good people find hard to resist, almost as if they are saying, "Hey, I grew up with a parent (or an older sibling) who never took my feelings and opinions seriously. I had to ask for their permission all the time and they rarely checked in to see how I viewed a situation. Now that I'm an adult, I don't want to have to stop and talk things over with someone who might disagree or slow me down. Sure it would be nice to have my partner's input, good ideas, and mutual consent before I rush into a major decision. But it's so much quicker to just do it my way and tell my partner later when it's a done deal."

For men, especially, it may feel unnatural and almost creepy to have to consult with your partner. You may have been told as a young boy—and may still be told—"Make up your own mind," "Don't be wishy-washy," "Be your own man." That's one of the reasons many men don't like to ask for directions or seek advice. From an early age they are taught it's weak, shameful, or downright unmanly to ask for consultation or advice when we should be making up our own minds as though we have all the answers.

For women there are different, but equally strong, reasons for not checking in with a partner. Some feel that they are giving the lover or spouse too much power, and that it's easier to get things done by not asking for input ahead of time. Other women were raised with the same tactics described in Nia Vardalos's *My Big Fat Greek Wedding*, where the mother teaches the daughter, "Do what

I do with your father—always make him think it was his idea and then he'll say yes." Still others were taught that you probably won't get a yes if you ask directly, but if you use your looks, your charm, or your sweet voice to distract your partner you will get the person to go along with what you want.

UDMs ARE THE WMDs OF RELATIONSHIPS

Unilateral (one-sided) decision-making might appear at first glance to save time or eliminate complicating factors, but over months or years in a romantic partnership, this attitude of "I'm gonna do what I want and you don't have any say in the matter" may slowly drive a wedge between the two of you and cause friction, hurt feelings, and ugly scenes. In fact, it may take years or decades to resolve the anger and loss of trust that occur when you pull a fast one on your partner and make a major decision without adequate consultation. I've counseled good people with good partners who have remained distant or distrustful of each other for many years after a Unilateral Decision-Maker, or UDM, left his or her partner out of a crucial decision.

Three types of UDMs are common:

The Pressured UDM makes a dinner commitment with an important client or a social engagement with friends and neglects to discuss it with his or her partner until the last minute. The Unilateral Decision-Maker will often say, "I felt pressured to do this." The left-out partner will often feel, "Bullshit! You could have said, 'Let me check with my partner to see if it works for both of our schedules. Then I'll get back to you by the end of the day.' " Do one or both of you sometimes make plans without considering the other person's preferences or needs?

The Generous-but-Controlling UDM buys his or her partner a new car, a piece of furniture, or an article of clothing but neglects to ask for input about the color, fabric, style, or features for the item that the unconsulted partner would be using most of the time. The generous-but-controlling partner often says, "But I wanted it to be a surprise" or "But it was on sale and I just happened to be in the store." The unconsulted partner often feels, "I don't want to sound ungrateful, but could you stop for a moment and think about whether *you* would want to spend several years with something important that has the wrong colors, fabric, style, and features for your particular tastes and needs? I thought we were going to make that decision together . . . as teammates."

(In situations like this one, I've found it's a good idea for the couple to take the item back and start the decision process again, with better consultation and teamwork this time. Otherwise, each time you look at the car, furniture, appliance, clothes, or expensive item that your partner chose without considering your point of view, it's likely to bring back feelings of resentment and imbalance. But if you take the bold step of getting your money back for the item that's been causing a rift between you, you will hear a wake-up call in your relationship that says, "We learned something here. We're going to be partners from now on and not pull any fast ones on each other. Our trust and our sense of teamwork are more important than this item that was driving a wedge between us.")

The Subtle UDM pretends to be flexible but really isn't. For example, when asked which restaurant or movie he or she might prefer, the Subtle UDM says, "Oh, it doesn't matter to me. Whatever you want is fine." But then when the initiating partner suggests a restaurant or movie, the unilateral decision-maker frowns and says, "No, I don't think so." The initiating partner may then offer a second choice of a restaurant or movie, to which the UDM frowns and says, "No, I'm not in the mood for that." Pretty soon, after three or four rounds of "whatever you want is fine, except for that and that and that," the initiating partner gives in and goes along with the particular movie or restaurant that will cause the subtle UDM to say yes, even if it's a movie or restaurant the initiating partner doesn't especially like. Does this sound familiar to you? Do you sometimes feel like a dentist pulling teeth to get your loved one to be flexible or to say yes without a huge ordeal?

The next time you or your loved one suspects that one of you is being a unilateral decision-maker, you don't need to scream or shout at each other. All you need to do is calmly and lovingly say to your partner, "Let's take a few minutes and admit what we each want or don't want regarding this decision. Then let's invent an imperfect solution that respects both of our differing points of view."

For example, let's say you and your partner are trying to pick a movie to see and you have different preferences in films. Maybe one of you likes romantic films and the other likes action-adventure. If you were in the mood to be a bit of a bulldozer, you could try to persuade and convince your partner to go along with your preference. Or if you were in the mood to be a whiner or martyr, you could go along 100 percent with your partner's choice and then try to guilt-trip your partner into letting you have your way the next time. Or if you were in the mood to be a unilateral decision-maker, you could order the tickets on-line and say to your partner, "Guess what we're going to see."

Or, if you'd like to have a great relationship and not add to the resentment that has been building, you could use the magic words, "Let's take a few minutes and admit what we each want or don't want regarding this decision. Then let's invent an imperfect solution that respects both of our differing points of view." Even if you think you're choosing on your own what you sense your partner would like, you need to remember that the majority of us would rather be consulted about life's important decisions.

"Just Those Few Words Made It Easier"

When I counseled Jayne and Brian, this simple solution led to a breakthrough in their relationship. For years, Jayne had been acting like a silent martyr, going along with Brian's choices regarding restaurants, films, and other seemingly minor decisions. But eventually she began to realize that her sense of resentment and emotional distance had been increasing with each accommodation. So, a few days after a counseling session, Jayne and Brian were trying to plan their date night together and she used the two sentences described above.

According to Jayne, "Just those few words made it easier for us to talk like equal partners instead of my being the pleaser and Brian being the one who needs to be pleased. When I said, 'Let's take a few minutes and admit what we each want and don't want,' something interesting happened. Brian admitted he didn't feel comfortable going to a violent action film with me because he knew it was going to make me feel shut down and distant afterward. And I admitted that I didn't want him to be bored sitting through one of my favorite foreign films or slow-moving romances because it made me uncomfortable to know that he was having a lousy time in order to accommodate my preference. So then we took turns coming up with 'imperfect solutions' that respected both his desire for a fast-action plot and my desire for deep and realistic characters. Within a few minutes, we came up with two films that had enough suspense and excitement to keep him interested and enough romance and character development to keep me happy. Not only did we have a much better date night than usual, but it set up a new way for us to make decisions as teammates instead of adversaries."

If you and your partner are both strong-willed people with differing opinions, I urge you to try out these two sentences the next time you are making a decision and see if they don't dramatically improve your sense of closeness and teamwork. Something remarkable happens when you warmly say to your loved one, "Let's make this decision together."

"Let's Make This Interesting for Both of Us"

Many people make the mistake of calling their partners all sorts of names that send them further into stubbornness, denial, or continued unilateral decision-making—names like "selfish" or "passive-aggressive." It doesn't matter whether these terms are practically or clinically accurate. The effect is that such words will put up an impenetrable wall between you.

On the other hand, I have found over the years that the people who are most successful at helping their partners stop the unilateral habit are the ones who avoid name-calling altogether and instead offer a healthy alternative.

A good example of this is Ellie, a writer and story editor for television, who is married to Howard, a decent but somewhat controlling financial services manager. Every so often Howard leaves Ellie out of major decisions, especially ones about which Howard senses that Ellie would have a differing viewpoint. For years Ellie called Howard "a control freak," which only prompted Howard to get defensive and insist, "I do tons for you and the family."

Then Ellie agreed to try something different. She decided almost a year ago to sit down with Howard and make him a deal. She said to her husband, "Let's make this interesting for both of us. How about every time you make an important decision without including me in the process, I get to spend a day at the spa getting a facial to soothe my angry eyebrows and a massage to relax my tense shoulders. And every time you successfully make sure to include me in a major decision, I'll give you a massage and who knows what else."

Howard smiled at her suggestion. He said, "You've got a deal."

During the past twelve months, Howard has slipped up only once, and, true to their agreement, Ellie got to spend the day in a spa. According to Ellie, "Except for that one minor relapse,

Howard has been excellent at including me in every important decision."

Ellie smiles mischievously as she wonders out loud, "Is it because he's too cheap to pay for a spa day for me? Or is it because he looks forward to my giving him a massage and maybe something more? Or is it perhaps that his empathy and his sense of fairness kicked in a bit and he's trying harder to be a great partner? I can't prove what his reasons might be, but I can say we're a lot closer and less argumentative now that he's broken his old habit of leaving me out of important decisions." Clearly, Ellie and her husband Howard found a way to break a long-time habit that had been hurting their relationship.

If the prospect of a spa day or a massage doesn't appeal to you or your partner, try something else that does. Just make sure you and your beloved avoid turning this issue of shared decision-making into an even worse power struggle of name-calling and defensiveness. I urge you to ask your partner, "What can we set up as an attractive incentive or an effective consequence to make some progress in changing this old habit?" The more you make it playful and enticing for both of you, the more likely you are to succeed.

THE NICE PERSON WHO REACHES THE BREAKING POINT

Now we come to the fourth and final problematic behavior that makes it difficult to achieve balance between being too flexible and not being flexible enough. I've seen this situation cause considerable heartache in hundreds of relationships. It happens when a nice person gives in over and over and then suddenly reaches a limit and becomes cranky or angry.

Has that ever happened to you? Have you ever been so helpful or accommodating for your partner or your kids that eventually you started to feel resentful or exhausted? Or have you ever given so much time and energy to your family, your work, or creative projects that you became irritable or impatient? Or have you tried so hard not to make waves with your partner that you began to feel taken for granted?

I hope you understand there's nothing wrong with being a nice person. But there is something problematic about a nice person who doesn't know how to ask for help, or delegate, or bring in someone for occasional relief. In fact, many good relationships are harmed or become tense because a nice person doesn't set healthy limits before *rather than after* he or she reaches a breaking point.

"I Have Trouble Saying No"

Consider the dilemma faced by Michael, one of my counseling clients, who is a highly creative graphic artist. Michael works extremely hard all week to keep his freelance graphics business going strong and to fight off new competitors who are trying to steal his best customers. So when the weekend arrives and his wife and children want to do things as a family, Michael often feels caught in a dilemma. As he describes it:

"By the time Friday night rolls around, I'm cooked. But I have trouble saying no, even when my wife Rita is asking me to do something I don't really wanna do. So if Rita asks me to run several errands on the weekend, or to take the kids to soccer and Sunday School and a friend's house for a play date, I'll often say yes just to be a nice guy. Then I end up resenting her later, which I realize is not the most mature and healthy thing to do.

"Then there's this other side of me, which I call the 'Don't mess with me' side of my personality. If I'm extremely tired after a busy week, or if I start doing too much for my wife and kids several weekends in a row, I get very cranky. Rita says she can tell when I've reached my limit because I start snapping at her or the kids. Last week I had a very stressful few days with pressing deadlines for three different customers who couldn't make up their minds about anything. Then on Saturday I took the kids to soccer practice and to McDonald's, where my four-year-old absolutely refused to get out of the maze of kid-sized tunnels that are too narrow for my big grown-up butt."

According to Michael, "There I was in front of about fifty people and I started shouting at my four-year-old to get out of the tunnel RIGHT NOW, but he totally ignored me. Pretty soon I was one of those out-of-control, cranky adults who definitely need to have their own time-out! It was embarrassing and it made me wonder, 'What the hell am I doing? How did I turn into one of those resentful, burned-out parents who have lost the ability to be playful and coax their kids out of a stupid climbing structure? My seven-year-old gave me a concerned look and said in a hushed voice, 'Dad, you need to chill. Your face is all red and you're not doing this right.'"

Like many decent and caring people, Michael knew how to work hard at his career and do a lot for his family. What he hadn't learned yet was how to take good care of himself so that he didn't go beyond his limits and lose his temper with his loved ones in public or in private.

During our next counseling session, Michael and I explored why so many "nice people" fluctuate between taking care of everyone else and burning out or becoming cranky. Sometimes the problem is that nice people don't want to disappoint anyone, so they say yes to too many requests and soon become exhausted and irritable. Or nice people don't even want to admit to themselves that they have limitations and breaking points. Even though Michael's wife and kids know that he isn't superhuman, he (or any nice person) often has trouble facing this humbling fact. Does this sound a little like you or your partner? Are one or both of you so "nice" and "giving" that it has started to lead to resentment or impatience?

Michael discovered that "taking care of everyone except myself is a habit I picked up long ago when I was a kid. I was the oldest child growing up with a hard-working, divorced mom who needed me to be responsible for keeping my four younger siblings out of trouble. I usually did what was necessary to keep the family going, but I often felt ripped off because everyone else was out having fun, and I was being the 'good kid' who handled way more than a child should have to handle."

Michael admitted he sometimes felt too guilty or responsible to say no to the errands, chores, or helping out that his adult family wanted him to do. So I asked Michael to think about the practical wisdom offered by flight attendants on commercial airlines: "In the event of an emergency, put on your own oxygen mask first before trying to help the person next to you."

For a compassionate person like Michael, that advice might seem counterintuitive. Michael and most "nice" men and women would automatically put the oxygen mask on their loved ones before attending to themselves. But here's what happens if you don't seriously consider your own needs regarding oxygen, weekend plans, errands, chores, help from others, or time for your own needs. If you focus only on the needs of others, you will quickly run out of oxygen, get disoriented, have muscle cramps, become cranky or impatient, and be ineffective in helping your loved ones. The reason to take care of your own oxygen first is to boost your capacity and endurance for coming through for others.

Using the story of the oxygen mask as a reminder that we all need replenishment in order to function well, Michael and Rita used their next counseling session to plan a new and improved way of choreographing weekend activities that respected each other's needs and ways of doing things. Instead of waiting for Michael to reach his burn-out point again, they agreed to take just fifteen minutes well in advance of the weekend to design a more balanced and sensible weekend plan.

Michael began the brainstorming session by admitting, "It's never been easy for me to ask for what I want because I don't like to appear weak or needy. But if I were going to design a perfect weekend, it would start with my catching up on some sleep on Saturday morning and then getting some exercise to feel energized.

Then I'd be willing to do a few hours of errands, chores, and driving the kids to their activities, as long as I knew that on Saturday night or Sunday night I'd get to have a relaxing 'date night' with Rita. And on these date nights I don't want some boring double date with another couple where we watch them argue or talk about trivia. What I want in order to feel alive and recharged each weekend is to go out to a nice restaurant, see a good film, and maybe even make out like hot teenagers with my wife in the car on the way home. Then we also need to schedule in half a day for some family activity and half a day catching up on some of our errands to get ready for the upcoming week."

I asked Michael if he'd ever been so clear and specific in describing his needs to Rita. Michael laughed and said, "No, my usual method has always been to pretend I'm invincible and then to snap when I reach my breaking point."

After we'd heard Michael's suggestions for an ideal weekend, it was time to ask Rita what would make her weekends more satisfying. Before she spoke, however, I gave them the advice I give everyone in brainstorming sessions: Whatever you do, don't shoot down your partner's ideas or try to win any arguments. This is just a chance to get your ideas on the table. After you've both had an uninterrupted first round, then you may start refining and designing a weekend plan that incorporates your differing needs. You both must avoid attacking, dismissing, and judging if you both want to feel included, respected, and treated fairly.

For the next several minutes, Rita listed some of the things she longed for on the weekends. She wanted at least a couple of hours alone with Michael, a couple of hours where the whole family was together doing something fun, educational, or spiritual, and finally a couple of hours to visit her aging parents (and on some weekends to see her older sister's family, too).

After she expressed all of these ideas without any backtalk or criticism, we then began to choreograph how to combine their diverse needs into successful weekends. Both Michael and Rita were surprised at how quickly the problem had shifted from an "I can never win at this" feeling of powerlessness to a positive sense of "We can design it as creatively and customized as we want." I've found with numerous couples that when they set up a weekly fifteen-minute planning meeting to ensure that their weekend needs get met, they prevent a huge amount of resentment and disappointment.

Several weeks later, during their final counseling session, Rita told me about the changes she had seen in Michael and in their relationship. "I always knew I'd married a decent guy. But I often worried about how he never seemed willing to admit ahead of time that he was starting to burn out or become cranky. I even thought a couple of times that our relationship was not going to survive if every weekend I had a short-tempered partner who couldn't ask for what he needed and who kept snapping at the kids and me.

"But during these last several weeks we've made an excellent plan for each weekend that includes the best of what I need and the best of what Michael needs in order to feel replenished, healthy, and more connected as a family. To my surprise, Michael was actually quite good at saying what he needs once we got into the habit of a quick fifteen-minute weekly brainstorming session.

Now instead of Michael doing too much and becoming miserable, he's been a real pleasure to be with on the weekends. We've had some great family moments and some terrific date nights. Our love life has also improved lately because we're getting along so much better. Now when Michael kisses me or holds me at night, I feel like I'm with an exciting lover again, instead of a burned-out and resentful 'nice guy.' "

PUTTING THESE IDEAS INTO PRACTICE

As Michael and the other men and women in this chapter have discovered, a lot can go wrong in your relationship if you drift too far in the direction of being too flexible or not flexible enough. But if you make an effort each day and each week to slightly adjust how you ask for what you need and how you listen to the needs of your loved ones, you will definitely find a more balanced way of living. You will achieve a much better connection to your spouse and to what nourishes your own soul.

One final comment: The next time your partner accuses you of being rigid, stubborn, or controlling, don't argue or ask your loved one to bring in more evidence. Just use this person's remarks as a wake-up call to begin to make some improvements in how you include others in your decisions and plans. Or if your partner accuses you of being too wishy-washy, indecisive, or people-pleasing, don't get defensive or shut down. Instead, use this opportunity to practice some of the tools described in this chapter to create a relationship that respects both of you.

Not only will your home life improve if you find a better way to balance self-care and compassion for each other's needs, but you will also be showing your kids, your extended family, and your close friends the importance of fairness and mutual respect. You will be modeling for the current generation and for future generations what a healthy partnership looks like so that they will know how to make it happen in their own lives. That might be one of the most important things you give to the people you care about and to those who are deeply affected by the way you and your partner treat each other. You will provide a living illustration of a balanced, harmonious, and strong relationship.

MAKING YOUR INTIMATE MOMENTS MORE SATISFYING

Are you feeling frustrated because one of you is often "in the mood" while the other often isn't? It's a dilemma that nearly every couple faces. During my twenty-three years of counseling couples, I've found that sexual tension resulting from differing sex drives is not simply due to men being men and women being women. I've discovered that two-thirds of the time it's a turned-on male who desires more sex than his partner, but I've also found that, in one-third of heterosexual couples, it is the passionate female who longs for an increase in lovemaking or an improvement in the quality of intimate moments. Quite often women tell me, "My partner used to be great in bed. But lately he's so consumed by his work that he never seems to have any energy or affection left over for our time together. That's sad, because I happen to enjoy making love. What I don't enjoy is the one-sidedness, the lack of romance, and the angry reactions I get when our sexual desires are out of sync."

I hear similar comments from same-sex couples. One of my counseling clients is Alicia, a physical therapist who's been in a ten-year relationship with a high-powered corporate executive named

Margaret. Alicia explains, "My partner Margaret tells me not to take it personally that she's lost the desire to be intimate lately. How do you not take it personally when night after night you get turned down? My beautiful companion is so stressed from work that she only wants to do crossword puzzles at night and drift off to sleep." A gay client named Martin, who's in a solid five-year relationship, told me, "My partner has been depressed lately and that sends his sex drive down to zero. There's a part of me that feels empathy for what he's going through and a part of me that wants to say, 'Enough already. Go see a psychiatrist and be sure to ask for the depression meds that don't squash your sex drive.'"

GETTING PERSONAL

So, please permit me to ask you a very personal question. How's your love life? The reason I'm asking is not to place blame on you or your partner. Rather, my intention is to help you and your partner get ready for some delicious lovemaking, grounded in the kind of exquisite intimacy that requires months or years of being in a relationship. That's right—I said you can have great sex in a long-term relationship. Many people simply don't believe that lovemaking can be increasingly wonderful year after year with the same partner. Fortunately, the skeptics are wrong.

I have seen repeatedly in my counseling practice and in my own life and circle of friends that there is a profound and passionate intimacy that couples can attain after many years together. Even though the widely held stereotype says that lovemaking is likely to become boring, repetitive, and less satisfying after several years with the same partner, I know many couples who experience sex as more fun and more amazing the longer they've been together.

If you are open to learning some specific ways to restore the tenderness and passion that may have been missing lately for you or your partner, then you've come to the right place. In this chapter I'll tell you how to improve the quality of intimacy between you and your partner, which is crucial for staying satisfied in a relationship. First we'll explore what to do when your sex drive differs from your partner's—and, maybe more important, what not to do. Then I'll offer some proven ways to get more of what you both want without hurting each other's feelings or getting defensive. If you and your partner take even a short amount of time to address these issues, then it's likely that your levels of passion, intimacy, and closeness will improve dramatically. I can't promise you that your lovemaking will be perfect. But I can say with at least 80 percent certainty, based on what I've seen with my counseling clients, that your love life with your partner will be stronger and more satisfying than it's been in a while.

INTIMACY ISSUES

Let's say you are feeling sexual and your partner wants nothing more than to catch up on sleep. This is where things get interesting for couples in committed relationships.

But before we start exploring how to improve your intimacy, we need to clarify the important difference between "obligatory sex," where one partner feels pressured, coerced, or less than satisfied, and "true intimacy," where both partners feel appreciated, energized, and deeply loved. In far too many relationships there tend to be several months or several years of obligatory sex. ("I'm not in the mood to make love, but I'll do it anyway so my partner will stop pressuring me.") This kind of sex might work for a while, but eventually one or both partners get tired of the lack of true closeness and, as a result, they begin to drift apart emotionally. Or they make negative comments and keep score ("We don't do it as often as everybody else").

Based on what I've seen from counseling hundreds of couples, there is a key warning of what not to do that I hope you will take seriously. On any given day or night, if you feel aroused and your partner doesn't, your brain and your emotions will probably want to start building a case against your partner. You might have thoughts like, "This isn't fair" or "How can you say you love me when you don't want to be with me the way I want to be with you?" Or you might feel like blurting out with some edge in you, "Do you know how long it's been since we've made love?" in the hope that your partner will feel guilty and stop turning you down so often.

Please permit me to be blunt about this. If you want someone to be interested in you sexually, don't start criticizing, complaining, or building a case against this person. It isn't sexy, and it won't lead to a mutually satisfying roll in the sheets.

Without a doubt, in some areas of life keeping score is essential. If you're playing cards or if you're adding up deductions for your tax forms, it's very important to keep close track of the numbers. But when it comes to lovemaking and long-term intimacy, the fastest and surest way to make the problem worse is to keep score in order to build a convincing case against your loved one for not making love often enough.

Think about it for a moment. If someone said to you, "I'm so frustrated! It's been nine friggin' days since we made love," would your response be, "Oh, darling, I feel all tingly and turned-on when you talk to me like that, with those sexy guilt trips of yours. Let's get naked." Or if someone said, "We used to make love 2.5 times a week, but now it's barely once a week [or once a month]," would the other person be likely to react by saying, "Oh, you hot little thing. I can't resist you when you talk quantitatively like that. Don't stop. Whatever you do, don't stop. . . ."

We live in a score-keeping society. Millions of us keep track of calories, cholesterol, carbs, pounds, and body measurements. We judge ourselves and others by the square footage of homes, the size of paychecks, and the grades and test scores of kids. In the same way, millions of couples incorrectly measure the success or failure of their relationship against how often they "do it." Unfortunately, I've found that, in more than 99 percent of my counseling cases, once one partner starts keeping score and building a case against the other partner, their sexual problem only gets worse.

THE MYTH UNDERMINING YOUR INTIMACY

I once attended a major professional conference dedicated to "Improving Sexuality," where one of the speakers lectured on how to get couples to live up to what he insisted was the "national norm" for sexual intimacy: 2.5 times per week. I have to admit that I had doubts about him the moment he cited that statistic. I still wonder if researchers can get people to be honest about how often they make love.

I raised my hand and asked, "Where exactly does that number come from?"

The speaker got defensive and said, "Well, everybody knows that 2.5 times per week is the average." Don't you love it when a stubborn person who doesn't have the facts says, "Well, everybody knows . . ."? Another therapist in the audience asked, "How can we be sure people are telling the truth about something so private?" The speaker got angry and replied, "Trust me. The average is 2.5 times per week." I thought to myself, why would anyone aspire to be average in bed anyway? And what exactly happens during that fractional .5 encounter? Does one person have an orgasm while the other partner thinks about going shopping? Does that .5 indicate they go halfway and then suddenly stop?

So I raised my hand again and asked, "What was the sample size of the research study where they found 2.5 times a week is the norm?"

The speaker became visibly angry. "It doesn't matter," he insisted. "The fact is if you're not getting some action at least two or three or even four times a week, your relationship stinks. Next question."

I mention this incident because the myth of a "national norm" for sexuality or a frequency of "doing it" score for relationships, which this speaker was perpetuating, is problematic for many couples. I have seen hundreds of decent and intelligent people in good relationships with great potential for wonderful intimacy get upset with themselves or their partners because they weren't meeting the rumored "average" of 2.5 times a week. I have seen countless couples argue about whether a beautiful love-making session once a week or once a month is sufficient for a great relationship because they've heard about someone down the street who claims to be exchanging bodily fluids five or six times a week. I have counseled too many couples who feel insecure about their own sexuality simply because they're not measuring up to some "norm."

During the refreshment break at this conference, I spoke with more than a dozen other therapists who were equally put off by the speaker's obsession with sexual quantity. Several told me, "I've always thought that the 2.5 number is nonsense." One therapist commented, "Especially when you've got kids and a busy life, I'd much rather have a delightful intimate connection a few times a month than to have a boring or mechanical 2.5 times per week."

WHAT TO DO WHEN YOUR SEX DRIVES DIFFER

Instead of keeping score or building a case about someone's lack of responsiveness, what else might you do when one partner is hot to trot and the other is tired, depressed, anxious, busy, or preoccupied with other things? The key is to focus on the *quality* of your love-making, not the quantity.

LEARN TO ENJOY THE ANTICIPATION

As nearly any tingly teenager can tell you, one of the most powerful things about sex is the longing for it—the mystery and unpredictability of when—and if—you're going to get it. Can you remember how excited and vibrant you felt with all that energy coursing through your body when, as an adolescent or young adult, you first started feeling the rush of sexual urges? Unfortunately, many lovers lose their feeling for the beautiful longing that days or weeks of desire can stir up, and instead start resenting and criticizing each other for the waiting and hoping that is a crucial and inevitable part of any sexual relationship. Quantity-focused partners may incorrectly assume that "love means never having to say you're sleepy." But your life partner is not an ATM machine, there for convenient depositing and withdrawing; or a high-speed computer that can hook you up in less than a second. Sexual intimacy is a delicate and fragile part of a complicated relationship. When both partners are in the mood, it can be wonderful, but a whole lot of factors can cause either one or both of you to slip out of the mood at any given moment.

For example, Jason is an athletic man in his thirties who admits, "My sex drive is much more intense than my wife Anna's. I would love to get it on with her at least four times a week, and she'd be happy if we did just one slow-motion, candlelit, romantic lovemaking per month. Sometimes I get frustrated and short-tempered from all the rejection."

The substantial difference in their sex drives, which began after they'd been married for several years and had had two children, was one of the reasons Jason and Anna called for some counseling. During their first session we began to explore what might help Jason be less short-tempered and what might help Anna warm up again to her husband.

To help Jason, I asked him two questions that every person with a high sex drive should consider: "When you get impatient and angry with Anna for being too tired at the end of a stressful day and saying no to sex, exactly how many days or weeks does that *add* to the time you won't be having any? Does your anger and impatience add one week, two weeks, or three weeks to the time you have to wait for Anna to feel sexual again?" Jason laughed and nodded his head in agreement. "You're right," he admitted. "Each time I get resentful or demanding, she pulls away for at least a week, maybe two."

Like most people I have counseled whose sexual needs are more intense than their partner's, the more Jason put pressure on his hesitant spouse, the more she tended to shut down sexually. It reminds me of the fascinating character played by Spike Lee in his first film, *She's Gotta Have It*, where he kept begging a less-than-interested partner, "Please baby, please baby, please baby, please!" That line was so recognizable to so many people in the audience that theaters nationwide began selling T-shirts that said PLEASE BABY, PLEASE BABY, PLEASE BABY, PLEASE! These words capture the desperation and intensity that many of us have experienced, but think about it—it's usually a turn-off for the partner.

Rather than seeking quantity with your hesitant or over-stressed partner, which only makes him or her shut down more, try another option: Honor the person for being courageous and honest enough to say no instead of faking it and saying yes. The hesitant partner, like Anna, is the one who needs tenderness and plenty of time to start desiring sex again. The highly sexual partner, like Jason, needs to slow down a bit and surrender to the mystery and the anticipation that is a part of any sexual relationship.

"If I Stop Pushing, There Won't Be Any Sex at All"

If you study various spiritual traditions, especially Tantric yoga, you will find that sexual energy is usually viewed as a precious life force, a profound gift from a higher source. In Tantric yoga you are encouraged to fully embrace the turned-on feelings and not to release them too quickly. Instead, feeling attracted to your lifelong partner is a chance to breathe deeply and send the sensual energy up and down your spine, to your head, arms, fingers, legs, and toes, rather than just your genitals. Feeling aroused or sensual about your beloved partner is viewed as something holy and beautiful, something to be enjoyed, rather than as an itch that needs to be scratched.

Several years ago I attended a "Sacred Sexuality" workshop where we learned precisely how to breathe, relax, slow down, and enjoy sexual energy for days and weeks at a time without having an orgasm. Let me tell you, it was a more energizing and exciting experience than almost anything else in life. Once you learn how to breathe and relax right at the moment the sensual energy starts to feel too strong for you, you will be amazed by how alive and vibrant you feel.

So I asked Jason, "Would you be interested in breathing in deeply the next time you feel turned on to Anna and just appreciating how alive you feel at that moment, even if there's no sexual contact? Would you be willing to let Anna set the pace for the next few weeks and months? It might be difficult at times to tell your body to hold on to your arousal and feel how it energizes your mind, your nerve endings, your muscles, and your heart, but this slowly simmering fire inside you will give Anna a chance to regain her desire and her sense of intimacy. It might also make you appreciate how attracted you are to her and how much you are willing to wait in order to be with her, which can be very romantic for both of you."

Jason was more than a little concerned about whether he could do this. Like most men, he'd been raised with the adolescent myth that he might get "blue balls" or succumb to some other terrible malady if he didn't have a quick release every time there was sexual energy streaming through his body. But, ultimately, he agreed: "If that's what we need, I'll try it."

Then I asked Anna, "Even if you decide not to go back to the four-times-a-week lovemaking that Jason remembers from when you first got engaged several years ago, what specific improvements in the relationship might help you be in the mood and say yes a little more often? You can ask for absolutely anything if it will help you to warm up again."

Anna thought for a moment and then looked directly at Jason and said, "Can I really ask for anything?" Jason appeared a little nervous. "Sure, you can ask for anything, unless it's more than I can afford."

Anna took his hand and said, "To be honest, what would really make me feel sensual again is not if you bought me stuff, but if you treated me lovingly in the other areas of our relationship besides our sex life. The more attentive and helpful you are to me and to the kids on a daily basis, the more I get the urge to be sensual with you in lovemaking. The more you're willing to be a good listener rather than becoming impatient or short-tempered, the more I can sense my body relaxing and feeling good when I'm around you."

She paused and looked down, a little worried about what she was going to say next. Then she took a deep breath and said, "Most of all, I need you to stop pushing so hard and pressuring me when you're in the mood and I'm not there yet. I know you're a very sexual person, but when you try to rush me or pressure me it blocks any chance I might have of warming up and feeling close to you."

At first Jason became a bit defensive. "Yeah, right. If I stop pushing, there won't be any sex at all."

But Anna took his hand again and looked him straight in the eyes as she said calmly, "Trust me on this. I do want us to have a great sex life, which means letting me unwind and heat up slowly. Because when you get angry or pressure me, it's that much more difficult for me to get the warm feelings flowing again."

I wasn't sure if Jason was going to take Anna's needs seriously or if he was going to stick with his old habits of pressuring and resenting. It's never easy for a person to change, and sometimes a frustrated individual won't truly listen to what the hesitant partner needs until the wall between them has grown so high and wide that they are close to a breakup.

Yet for the next several weeks, Jason *did* make a conscious effort to be more loving and helpful in all areas of their marriage, and at the same time he let Anna warm up slowly without criticizing or pressuring her. Like many intelligent people with a strong sex drive, Jason was willing to lighten up rather than make things worse by being stubborn or demanding.

For Anna, this was the beginning of a major change in how she viewed sexuality. She explained, "Ever since I was a teenager and my body began to develop, boys and men have been pushing me to go faster than I was comfortable with, and not really listening to what I needed. The fact that Jason has started to slow down somewhat and respect my feelings has made me a lot more in love with him lately."

As a result of both partners shifting slightly from their old ways, a renewed sensuality began to take place in their marriage. As Anna described, "Because I'm noticing Jason's caring and respect more often, I feel a lot more affectionate and relaxed around him. In response, we've had some wonderful lovemaking sessions lately. Maybe not as often as Jason might prefer, but a lot more than we've had since the kids were born."

Jason added, "I'm never quite sure when Anna is going to warm up, and there's something exciting and awesome about being in that risky state of anticipation and desire. I'm a guy who has to push a lot and pressure people in order to be successful in my work, in my training at the gym, and in many of my personal relationships. But with Anna, I'm finding there's a sensuality to just treating her well and watching how it slowly results in her getting in the mood.

During the last few weeks we've only made love a couple of times, but each time has been amazing because I could sense Anna was 100 percent there with all of her energy and emotion."

DIY—WHEN TO "DO IT" YOURSELF

If one person in a couple wants sex several times a week and one person wants to make love less frequently, another option is to talk to each other about self-pleasuring, masturbating, or developing a form of self-caressing that you might enjoy together.

For many couples it's difficult to talk about masturbation, or to admit to your partner what you do when you're pleasuring yourself. Yet if you can initiate a nonjudgmental and creative brainstorming conversation with your beloved about the various possibilities of going it alone, specifically for those days or nights when only one of you is in the mood, it can take a lot of the pressure off—and the arguing out of your love life.

The conversation itself can be a deepening of your intimacy and closeness. When a woman tells her partner what feels good when she's pleasuring herself, it may help the partner understand how to give greater pleasure. For many women, masturbation with her own gentle hand, with a steadily flowing bath faucet, with a trusty vibrator, or with a flexible pillow can be a breakthrough that helps her discover her own comfort with her body and her sexuality. In the mid-1970s, I worked for Doubleday in New York when their groundbreaking book *For Yourself* was published. This caring and thoughtful guide by a respected sex therapist, Dr. Lonnie Barbach, helped millions of women discover how to deepen their comfort with their own sexual rhythms by exploring various methods of gentle self-pleasuring. Rather than learning about their sexual responses through the sometimes clumsy or rushed intensity of their partner, many women learned through self-pleasuring the pace, touch, rhythms, and settings that made them feel intimate and relaxed. Then they helped their partner replicate a similar rhythm, response, or romantic setting during their mutual lovemaking.

For example, one of my counseling clients is a woman named Rachel who grew up uncomfortable with her sexuality because she had been molested by an uncle when she was eleven years old. Rachel wanted to enjoy sex in a loving relationship, but her body would invariably tighten up and her thoughts would wander to painful memories. Only when Rachel began to explore self-pleasuring in the privacy of her own bathtub or in bed with a favorite vibrator did she begin to experience the joyful feelings of strong sexual arousal and complete release. After several weeks of experimenting on her own with what made her feel aroused and what helped her soar into heights of pleasure, she began teaching her husband how to assist her in replicating these blissful moments. For the first time in their marriage, the idea of sex for Rachel changed from a painful obligation to an extremely pleasurable shared intimacy.

"I'm Not Looking at These Women as Alternatives to Her"

For most men and many women, masturbation is a quick way to relieve the tensions of daily living and be open to the next time that both partners are in the mood for actual lovemaking. Rather than snapping at your partner with comments like, "We don't have enough sex anymore," you can simply balance out your differing sex drives with an occasional solo session or by a self-pleasuring that you invite your partner to watch or participate with you in a relaxed way.

A few warnings, however. The problem for many men and some women is that masturbation can become addictive. Recent research studies show that a surprisingly large number of men and a smaller number of women become so habitually attracted to pornography in magazines and on videos and the Internet that they begin to drift away emotionally from their real-life loved one. Or they start comparing their sufficiently attractive partner with the off-the-charts surgically altered or chemically enhanced bodies of the men and women they see in pornography. In many relationships where intimacy has been lacking, if a partner gets too accustomed to the predictable rhythms and rituals of masturbation, he or she may lose patience with or curiosity for the unpredictable and more complicated reality of human contact.

If you notice (or if your partner suggests to you) that pornography is creating a problem in your relationship, avoid it for a while to see if you can regain your interest in genuine person-to-person intimacy. Rather than staying dependent on pornography that offends your partner or that causes arguments, try instead to use your own rhythmic breathing, sensitive touch, and creative imagination. Or ask your partner to assist your arousal a bit without requiring him or her to exert much effort.

For example, Bruce and Diane are somewhat religious individuals who felt conflicted about Bruce's long-time dependence on pornography for his frequent masturbation. When they first entered counseling, Bruce was feeling defensive. "Diane is seriously on my case to give up the magazines and videos. What she doesn't understand is that I'm not looking at these women as alternatives to her. They're just beautiful bodies that get me going so I can relieve the daily tension that I don't want to impose on Diane."

Diane countered, "I'm not a prude, but I do think there's something wrong about Bruce obsessively buying these magazines and films and staring at other women's body parts. I asked Bruce to stop bringing this stuff into our home, especially since the kids are old enough now to find it and be confused by it. But lately Bruce is just getting more sneaky about maintaining his stash of magazines and videos."

Over the next few weeks during their counseling sessions, Bruce and Diane developed a creative solution to their disagreement. They decided to explore other ways of masturbating besides using pornography. Diane admitted to Bruce how much she enjoyed sitting in a candlelit tub with scented bath oils and letting the lukewarm water flowing from the faucet stimulate her to a slow and magnificent orgasm. Since he's often a generous and kind person, Bruce offered to help Diane by buying some candles, keeping the scented bath oils well-stocked, and giving her a before-the-bath neck massage and thirty minutes of privacy from the kids and other responsibilities.

In return, Diane offered to give Bruce a neck massage, or to curl up next to him with some low-exertion, sensual body contact a few times a week while Bruce pleasured himself, or to get him started and let him do the heavy lifting on his own during those nights when she felt tired or not in the mood for a full lovemaking session. Rather than putting distance between them, Diane and Bruce's brainstorming conversations about various solo practices created greater intimacy and trust. This intimacy resulted in more creative and satisfying lovemaking several times a month.

TAKE TURNS AS GIVER AND RECEIVER

A third way to stop clashing or bickering about your differing sex drives is to discuss ahead of time which of you has a lot of energy on a particular day or evening and which of you feels tired or not quite in the mood. Then, without judging or criticizing each other, simply choose to let the energetic partner do most of the passionate activity this time while the less-energetic partner practices the fine art of receiving.

For many couples, this conscious decision to be the primary giver and the primary receiver leads to some delicious lovemaking. To know that your partner is fully receiving your affections and not feeling pressure to perform or work hard during this particular session can free the giver to just give and the receiver to just receive. Ideally there will be a role reversal at some point in the next few days or weeks—when today's giver becomes a receiver and today's receiver becomes a giver. But for now, just enjoy the fact that you love each other and that you're honest and intimate enough to let each other know when you've got energy and when you don't.

"It Feels Great That We're No Longer Faking It"

Gillian's case is a good example of the breakthrough that can occur by taking turns being the giver and the receiver. Gillian grew up the eldest child in her family and has always been the hard worker who takes care of younger siblings, stray cats, disgruntled co-workers, and anyone else who needs a supportive friend. In addition, Gillian has a husband named Luke and four children, one of whom has special needs and requires a lot of assistance.

So when Luke asks Gillian, "Are you in the mood for some tenderness tonight?" Gillian's first thought is usually, "You've got to be kidding. I'm toast."

But a few months ago during a counseling session, we discussed the possibility of Gillian being a passive receiver on the nights when she's feeling tired and Luke is feeling amorous. At first Gillian was unsure of whether it might be "a bit tacky to relax and do very little while Luke does most of the strenuous fire-building." But Luke reassured her, "I might actually be having a good time, so I think we should give it a try once in a while."

Gillian laughed and said, "I'll try it once and if the idea of being generously cared for is too much for my workaholic brain to handle, you've got to let me complain a little about how strange and unfamiliar it is for me."

As a result of this playful but practical conversation, Luke and Gillian began a new phase of their intimate life. For the first time that Gillian could recall, she let herself breathe, relax, and do relatively little every so often during their lovemaking. She did feel a little guilty for a few moments, but reported later, "It was so incredible. I never fully realized just how much I'm doing, doing, doing all the time—taking care of everyone but myself. So when I felt Luke's love and his willingness to occasionally be the primary giver with no expectations that I reciprocate right away, I got tears in my eyes. It feels like one of the most caring gifts I've ever received."

Once again, if you and your partner experiment with these giver and receiver roles, you will need to do some additional brainstorming about how to make sure it feels fair and balanced to both of you. In Gillian's case, she suggested that since she felt most relaxed and energetic on Sunday mornings after Luke had gotten up with the kids and let Gillian sleep late, there might be a few Sunday mornings or afternoons each month where she would be the giver and Luke could be the passive receiver.

As Luke described, "I always knew that Gillian was feeling burdened by sex and that this feeling of resentment was starting to drive a wedge between us. But once we began to admit honestly to each other when we're tired and when we're feeling energetic, something changed about our lovemaking. Now I can sense that Gillian truly has learned how to relax and let me do more of the build-up when she's tired, while she becomes quite active and pretty creative on those occasional days when she's well-rested and energetic. It feels great that we're no longer faking it or hiding the truth from each other. It feels a lot more intimate lately between us."

HOW TO IMPROVE YOUR LOVEMAKING WITHOUT GETTING DEFENSIVE

Now that we've worked through the issue of sexual frequency, it's time to explore the sexual choreography clashes that can make or break your relationship. Specifically, have you ever tried to tell your partner what feels good during lovemaking and what you don't like, what feels too rushed as opposed to what feels warm and connecting? Maybe you have and, instead of replying, "I'm glad you told me," your partner responded with anger or defensiveness, as if you had criticized him or her. Or maybe you have noticed yourself feeling somewhat attacked, invalidated, or interrupted when your partner started making comments and suggestions during lovemaking. Did you ever say, or think about saying, "Oh, shut up already. Can't we just do this without all the commentary?"

Giving and receiving sexual feedback is a delicate and crucial issue for most couples. It's sad that many times a wonderful, intimate connection gets thwarted by a well-meaning comment that gets misinterpreted. Maybe all you said was "a little slower" or "a little more to the right," but your partner heard, "You stupid idiot, how could you be so clumsy?"

If we could each read our partner's mind and know exactly what he or she desired at every moment, there wouldn't be a problem. Couples with perfect knowledge of each other's sexual thoughts and feelings could just get hot and heavy without ever having a misunderstanding. But the truth is that no one can know exactly what you like or don't like from moment to moment. No matter how much you love each other, it's still quite likely that on any given night or day you might prefer to be touched a little slower, a little more unpredictably, a little to the left, or a little to the right. How do you make sure those choreography suggestions are expressed gracefully and received nondefensively? Here are five specific things you can do with your partner to keep your love life improving year after year:

TAKE A TWO-MINUTE TIME-OUT

Rather than criticizing your partner during the heat of lovemaking or keeping silent and putting up with sexual interactions that make you feel uncomfortable or disappointed, try this alternative to move your physical intimacy from passable to outstanding. All it takes is for one of you to call a two-minute time-out, either before you start getting intimate or as a brief interlude during the slow build-up or foreplay of your passionate moments together.

In a calm and uncritical tone of voice, say something like, "Can we take a two-minute time-out—I want to show you something I think is wonderful that I'm pretty sure you'll also enjoy." At that moment, your partner can choose either to say, "Would love to— you be the choreographer, I'll be your number one dancer," or "How about in a few minutes?" It's very important to make room in your lovemaking for one or two of these brief refining moments, because they can take your intimacy to much greater heights.

Then whether the two-minute time-out happens immediately or in a few minutes, make sure it becomes a caring, uncritical, and helpful demonstration rather than a rant, a put-down, or a preachy lesson. For example, I once counseled a married couple who had stopped making love because Bret, the husband, felt irritated and defensive when Cara, his wife, interrupted their intimate moments to give him suggestions. He became especially frustrated when Cara tried to offer a few comments about the way he kissed her. Bret commented during their counseling session, "Every other woman I've been with has told me I'm an incredible kisser. But not my wife—all Cara does is criticize me and try to control my every move."

"After a Minute or Two It Started to Get Pretty Hot in Here"

Like many partners who wish they could offer their loved one a few helpful tips about intimacy, Cara felt disappointed that her husband seemed unwilling to let her guide him on how she likes to be kissed. She explained, "It doesn't really matter whether Bret's ex-wife and his former girlfriends liked to be kissed in a certain way. I can't believe he wouldn't want to spend some time trying to find out how his current wife and genuine soul mate likes to be kissed. Every human being is different, and I happen to love a slow, exploratory, taking-turns kind of kiss rather than the abrupt, jam-the-old-tongue-down-the-throat kind of kiss that Bret thinks is so sexy. Maybe if he would just try out my way of gently exploring the lips, the insides, and the tongue with extremely slow and deliberate movements at first, then I might be able to get into the fast and furious stuff after a while."

Bret rolled his eyes and commented, "With Cara, it's always

about control. She's got to have complete control or else she shuts off."

While Bret and Cara were a little more outspoken than most couples about their different ways of kissing, I have found with the majority of long-term and committed partners that there are huge differences and unique preferences regarding how each individual likes to be kissed. Rather than ignoring each other's likes and dislikes, the most successful couples are those who take a brief two-minute time-out every few weeks or months to clarify for the other what they desire and what they don't enjoy.

When I asked Bret and Cara, "Would you be willing to take two minutes right now to show each other how you like to be kissed? Not in a critical or bossy way, but in a gentle and caring way, like a terrific choreographer gently and lovingly guiding his or her most cherished dancer. I'll leave the room for five minutes so you can have privacy. Are you interested?"

Cara and Bret looked at me with disbelief. Bret asked, "You want us to choreograph a kiss?"

"Absolutely," I replied. "An ideal kiss. The kind you've been wishing your partner would do all these years, but you've never quite been able to find the right words and the right relaxed setting in which to demonstrate it to each other. We'll let Cara go first and then when she's showed you her preference, it'll be your turn to describe or demonstrate the kind of kiss you've always desired."

Cara was concerned. "What if Bret thinks I'm being controlling or critical again? I don't want to provoke his anger and defensiveness—I've seen it far too often."

I turned to Bret and asked, "Would you be willing just for this two-minute time-out to imagine Cara to be the most gifted and brilliant choreographer in the world? She knows exactly what will make the most successful and satisfying choreography of her ideal kiss. Would you be willing to let her guide you in learning this amazing smooch?"

Bret smiled and said, "What have I got to lose? She hasn't wanted to kiss me for months. This could be a guaranteed moment of closeness."

Cara looked in my direction and said, "Do we really get five minutes of privacy?"

I replied, "Do you want more than five minutes?"

Cara laughed. "Nope, I think five minutes might be enough. We'll let you know when it's safe to come back into the office."

As often happens with couples who are seeking to regain the closeness and trust that has drifted out of their marriage, Cara and Bret were nervous at first when I left the room. But Cara told me a few minutes later, "It was such a relief to know that this was a short time-out solely for the purpose of demonstrating something important to each other. Neither one of us felt criticized or put down. We just took turns showing each other exactly the kind of kiss we've always desired."

Bret added, "I actually enjoyed the slow, exploratory, taking-turns kiss that Cara showed me. At first I didn't feel very much intensity from it, but after a minute or two it started to get pretty hot in here. Either your air conditioning isn't working very well, or Cara truly knows something about how to kiss."

I strongly urge you and your partner to find a quiet moment before lovemaking or during lovemaking to take turns having a nonjudgmental, nonattacking two-minute time-out for showing each other how you like to be kissed, how you like to be stroked, how you like to be held, how you like to be stimulated, and how you like to be soothed. Sure, it's a little uncomfortable to be talking about this private, vulnerable stuff with another person. But for God's sake, this is your soul mate who loves you and with whom you are building an ever-increasing intimacy. Your deep concern for each other and the substantial time already spent together have established a strong enough foundation—now it's time to let your partner know what you truly desire.

It's crucial, however, that you make sure these two-minute choreography demonstrations don't turn into sarcasm, hurtful comments, or one-upmanship. Simply treat your loved one as a cherished star dancer who only needs some gentle coaching from an extremely patient and supportive choreographer. Rather than hoping your partner will magically guess what you like without your having to say anything, use these caring two-minute time-outs every so often to deepen your intimacy and closeness.

TALK HONESTLY ABOUT HOW YOUR PLUMBING WORKS

If you have ever felt insecure that your body is imperfect or that it's not cooperating fully during lovemaking, I say welcome to the human race! Sooner or later, every long-term relationship will bump up against some plumbing concerns that, instead of being embarrassing secrets, can be opportunities for deepening your intimacy and trust with each other.

For example: Bill and Jake have been together for four years and recently Bill has had some erection problems. Jake's first reaction was, "He's probably found a new lover and he's not telling me about it."

Yet during a counseling session, Bill insisted, "I have no interest in finding someone else. I love the time we spend together and the home we're creating. My problem is that whenever I've been in a relationship more than three years, my arousal goes down somewhat. It doesn't mean that Jake and I aren't meant to be lifelong partners. It just means I need a lot more tenderness and stimulation to get going."

Like many men—heterosexual, gay, or bisexual—who are more easily turned on during the early phases of a relationship, Bill was frustrated with his erection difficulties. But as a result of their openly telling each other about the underlying issues, Jake and Bill designed a whole new sexual choreography that not only increased their physical intimacy but also strengthened their emotional closeness.

As Jake told me during their final counseling session, "The fact that Bill was willing to talk this over with me and explore various ways to revive our sex life was a huge breakthrough for us. Now we've got a much stronger trust and closeness than we did during the first few years when we were just mindlessly grabbing each other all the time but didn't really know each other. Now even on the nights when Bill has trouble getting hard or staying hard, there are so many other ways to bring each other pleasure. It's become a total nonissue."

In some cases a person with erection difficulties or arousal problems needs to see a physician to find out if there are medical reasons for the lack of response. There are major breakthroughs happening in the field of sexual medicine and alternative therapies to help men and women who have struggled with arousal problems, but you will need a qualified professional to help you sort out the possible side-effects, as well as the pros and cons of various treatments.

Or you might want to explore with a knowledgeable counselor the underlying reasons for your tendency to be attracted to newness and mystery while having trouble feeling turned on by a long-term partner who knows you well. I've found that these issues can be resolved with counseling, especially if you and your partner stop criticizing each other for the complexities of your sexual responses and start appreciating that every human being has challenges to work through regarding intimacy.

"It Wasn't His Fault That I Needed to Pull Away Sometimes"

Women also have plumbing issues that can be resolved if they and their partners talk about them openly and develop some innovative choreography to address them. For example, Jennifer and Carlos are a couple in their late forties. They were both divorced with kids of their own when they met six years ago and began dating. Their sex life was passionate during the first few years.

But something changed when Jennifer began experiencing perimenopausal symptoms. "I had always been a very sensual person, but when I hit my late forties I went through twelve months of hot flashes, agitation, vaginal dryness, and mood swings that completely turned me off to the idea of anyone touching me or expecting me to be sexual," she said. "I felt terribly guilty because Carlos is a good-looking man and a very fine husband. But I just couldn't make my body relax enough to enjoy making love. And I noticed that the more I said no or "not tonight" without much explanation, the more Carlos was starting to drift away emotionally. Pretty soon we both got busy with our jobs and we hardly found time any longer to be alone or to share any intimate moments."

Then Carlos and Jennifer decided, after attending a workshop I gave at their church, that they would set aside a few minutes each week to talk about how they were feeling physically and emotionally, what they needed from each other, and how they could be allies rather than adversaries in dealing with the perimenopausal symptoms. Instead of trying to hide their physical issues, they made a promise to brainstorm ways to help each other with the changes their bodies experienced, now and in the future. They began to design a new sexual choreography that could address issues like dryness, hot flashes, agitation, and mood swings.

As Jennifer recalls, "Those weekly conversations were such a relief. I no longer had to feel ashamed or hide from Carlos some of the things that were affecting me so strongly. I explained carefully to him why it wasn't his fault when I needed to pull away sometimes. We also talked about what kinds of touch and intimacy do feel good during my hot flashes and agitation. Now I enjoy his foot massages, his hand gently resting on my stomach, his gentle kisses on my back and arms, and his cooling me off with his tongue and his breath on my skin. I'm still not in the mood for intercourse. But it feels so intimate and loving when we have one of our gentle, erotic sessions once or twice a week, and I get to watch at the end while Carlos strokes himself to a passionate orgasm while I sip on a delicious cool glass of iced herbal tea. Sometimes it even feels like this improvised and unconventional lovemaking is a much deeper and more intimate connection than the old routines we did without much consciousness during our earlier years."

REVEAL HOW YOUR PARTNER CAN ASSIST (OR DISRUPT) YOUR ORGASMS

Isn't it amazing that so many couples never explain to each other exactly what works and what doesn't work for bringing them to satisfying orgasms? Even in basically good relationships, many women and some men suffer in silence when a partner finishes too soon or does something unintentional that interrupts the other person's impending orgasm. Or the woman fakes her orgasm with as much creativity as Meg Ryan's character in *When Harry Met Sally*. Or she has sadness in her heart month after month, year after year, as she says to her partner after nonorgasmic lovemaking, "Oh, it was great. I'm fine." A sizeable number of couples get into arguments about whether someone is "taking too long" to reach orgasm, as if the person with the slower response is doing it on purpose.

Rather than fighting or arguing about the search for elusive orgasms, you can discuss the issue calmly. The technique that works best is to set aside twenty minutes every few months or so to discuss nonjudgmentally, "Here's what I've learned works best for me to have a great orgasm and here's what I've learned can mess it up in an instant."

It's not about blame or who's a better lover. Even if you've been together for five years, twenty-five years, or longer, there might still be valuable clues to each other's orgasmic intricacies that you just haven't shared. Since every human being has a slightly different way of navigating the complicated muscle contractions, intense physical stages, and shifting emotions that occur before, during, and just after orgasm, it's crucial that you and your partner talk about this rather than assuming that because your partner loves you, he or she will just know what you need. Even the most considerate and caring partner can never know exactly what you need, what feels great, and what feels like a frustrating interruption during the intense moments of passionate lovemaking.

For example, Connie is a bisexual woman in her early thirties who recently celebrated her fifth year with her current partner. Connie told me in one of her counseling sessions that she was surprised to find out from personal experience that even the best lovers still don't quite know what she needs right at the moments leading up to and after an orgasm.

According to Connie, "When I was in high school and college

I dated a few men who were very experienced and claimed to be quite skillful in bed. But there still were a lot of moments when they were doing what they thought I wanted and yet it wasn't quite what my body needed. I didn't want to sound demanding or high maintenance, so I never really explained to them exactly what they could do differently to help me have an earth-shaking orgasm."

Connie then described how, during her early twenties, she began exploring her bisexual nature. "I started dating some truly wonderful women. I assumed they would know instinctively what intensifies the sensations prior to orgasm for a woman, and what kind of indirect and nonclitoral stimulation works best immediately after a huge release. Yet I discovered to my surprise that even the most tender and empathic women still didn't quite know exactly what I needed moment to moment."

"From That Day On Our Lovemaking Has Been Incredible"

Like many women, Connie was uncomfortable with the notion of having to talk about her most intimate needs with a partner. She admits, "I was hoping I could find a way to make everything turn out fine sexually without having to ask directly for what I might need." But after counseling to work through her concerns about being too demanding in a relationship, Connie took some time every couple of months to have a relaxed heart-to-heart conversation with her partner about what each of them liked or didn't like during the intense moments surrounding orgasm.

Connie explained, "These turned out to be some of the most fun conversations I've ever had with anyone about anything. To have an unpressed and intimate talk about orgasms with the person you love the most—it's surprisingly fabulous. We weren't criticizing or blaming each other for not being mind readers. We were finally admitting to each other some extremely helpful clues as to the timing and intricacy of what we each need most in order to have the best releases imaginable. From that day on our lovemaking has been incredible. It's sad to think it took me this long to open up and tell someone what really goes on for me around orgasms."

A similar situation existed for Gabriel, a highly sexual man in his late thirties who told me he has never felt comfortable enough to explain to his wife what he prefers most in order to heighten his orgasms. According to Gabriel, "Before I was married and I was dating all sorts of women, I found that several of them were able to do the particular things that bring me to the most satisfying climaxes. Yet I didn't want my wife to know just how experienced and sexually driven I am, so I kicked back and just settled for some less-than-satisfying lovemaking."

But Gabriel has worked for several months in counseling to explore and resolve his issues about how he was raised to view sexuality as "nasty" and to put women in categories of "good girls" and "bad girls." I urged him to read some books about how his particular religious denomination viewed sexuality, and he soon realized that a committed, monogamous sexuality could be quite passionate and sacred at the same time. As a result, he no longer felt he had to hide his intense physical nature from his wife.

So Gabriel finally got up his nerve and had a heart-to-heart talk with his wife about the things he enjoyed most and would love to try in their lovemaking. He told me afterward, "To my surprise, my wife wasn't shocked or offended. In fact, she's got a bit of a wild side of her own that she had also been hiding from me. She did say, however, that three of the five things I was requesting were not comfortable for her. But we've had a tremendous amount of fun lately from adding the two things that did intrigue and excite her."

When you do have an intimate conversation with your loved one about what you each need and prefer regarding orgasm, please accept that your partner has every right to say no to anything that doesn't feel safe, comfortable, or enjoyable. This is not a time for pressuring or guilt-tripping your partner into doing something that will eventually make you feel distant or resentful toward each other. Rather, it's an opportunity to increase your closeness by exploring whether there are a few fine points of lovemaking that you each can bring to the relationship in order to respect your unique and particular ways of reaching the heights of pleasure. Please consider that it's not "demanding" or "high maintenance" to calmly tell your partner what could deepen your love and enjoyment of each other. It's just sensible.

THE ORAL SEX CONTROVERSY—YOU GET TO DECIDE

There's another important aspect of sexual choreography that needs to be considered when you and your partner have a criticism-free conversation about your needs regarding orgasms. I have found as a therapist that approximately 70 percent of women receive their best orgasms through oral sex, and yet close to 40 percent of heterosexual men and 20 percent of lesbian women either refuse to give or are clumsy at giving oral sex. Some research studies say that 60 percent of women don't have an orgasm from intercourse and need oral sex for a complete orgasm, while other studies have estimated that the percentage of women who prefer receiving oral sex is as high as 80 percent.

Fifty or more years ago there were judgmental and misinformed "experts" who called women "frigid" if they didn't have an orgasm from intercourse. Now we know from talking to millions of women about this issue that it's perfectly normal, and far more common, for the majority of women to prefer oral sex over intercourse for reaching their best orgasms.

If you or your partner don't find intercourse to be the best way to bring about a satisfying orgasm, please don't think it means you're neurotic or holding back because of a psychological block. In most cases it simply means you're perfectly normal.

So the question is asked in many relationships, "Does a woman have the right to urge her partner to learn how to pleasure her with oral sex, even if the partner is uncomfortable, a bit awkward, or slightly impatient at first?" Should the couple just settle for a less-than-satisfying sex life and focus instead on the other good qualities of the relationship? Or is it okay for a woman to say to her partner, "I'd be happy to have intercourse if we first make sure you give me an unrushed, sensual, loving orgasm in the way that works best for me?"

I can't tell you and your partner what to do—those intimate decisions are completely up to you. But I can offer my personal and professional opinion as to what can definitely move your relationship from mediocre to outstanding. In many counseling sessions with individuals who were hesitant, clumsy, or rushed about oral sex, I say, "There's no law or constitutional amendment requiring oral sex in any of the fifty states or Canada. But let me tell you what I've heard from hundreds of couples. There are two ways to give oral sex to the woman in your life who truly enjoys and prefers it. The first way is to be in a hurry and to try to rush her into having a release. The second way is for you to enjoy the closeness, the intimacy, the slowness, the lack of pressure, the generosity, the surrender, and the ecstasy that can happen when you let her know you're completely in love with her and that you're in absolutely no hurry because this is one of the most luxurious and sensual things that two people can do. You decide which of these two approaches will strengthen your relationship and your home life."

A sensible partner will realize, "This is important. I need to do better at this." But occasionally I do meet a man who says, "I just can't be subservient to a woman and go down on her like that," or a man or a lesbian who admits, "I just can't slow down long enough to do it right." My experience has been that in more than 50 percent of the cases where someone continues to be reluctant, clumsy, rushed, or impatient about oral sex, the less-than-satisfied partner is either thinking about a breakup or taking steps toward a breakup. But hey, like I said earlier, it's not my decision. Ultimately, it's up to you.

SMOOTH OUT THE INITIATION OF INTIMACY

I conclude this chapter with two additional fine points of love-making that I've seen help shift couples from a so-so to a spectacular love life. The first is something that I often hear good and decent men wish could be improved about their relationships. As most men and some women have explained to me in counseling sessions, "It's difficult to always be the one to do the initiating. It's frustrating to be the one who gets turned down time after time, but when I ask my partner if she would be willing to take the risk and initiate sex once in a while, she rarely does."

When it comes to your own relationship, is there one partner—male or female—who usually does the initiating or the asking, or who makes the risky first move? Has the situation become so one-sided that one of you has started to get resentful?

What I recommend is not to fight or bicker about this imbalance, but to have a creative and nonattacking conversation instead. A relaxed and playful talk about how to bring more mutuality and teamwork to your love life is bound to be more effective than a rant or a tirade. The best solution I've seen is to set aside twenty minutes on a good day or night every few months to clarify:

* What are some of the subtle or obvious clues that your partner is comfortable giving you which would let you know ahead of time that he or she is sufficiently interested and will probably say yes?

* What are clues that your partner is willing to give you that he or she is a definite no for today or tonight?

❋ What are the clues your partner tends to give you that he or she is possibly interested, *if* you coax gently or warm him or her up?

Admitting to each other in a relaxed and nonjudgmental conversation how to read each other's clues is essential if you want to break out of the rut of "I always initiate and you don't" that happens in many relationships.

"I Don't Like to Come Out and Say, 'I'm in the Mood!'"

One of the couples I counseled recently are Brenda and Stephen, who have been together for almost ten years. They've watched their sex life change from hot and sweaty before they had children to "he's still asking but she's almost never saying yes" for the past two years.

When Brenda and Stephen took a romantic walk along a hillside trail near their home and admitted to each other what clues they each tend to send out that tonight might be yes, no, or maybe, they were each amazed at how often they hadn't known what to look for from their long-time partner.

Stephen was surprised to find out that Brenda often put her hand softly and lovingly on top of his hand at dinner on nights when she was feeling a little bit affectionate and was hoping he'd coax her with a first move and a gradually accelerating intimacy. Stephen commented, "I was so surprised to hear that this was one of Brenda's major clues that she might be feeling amorous. I always thought when she put her hand on my hand it meant she wanted me to stop talking or to lower my voice in the restaurant."

Brenda explained, "I don't actually want Stephen to have to be the initiator all the time. That's not fair to him and I wouldn't want to be in his shoes having to get turned down so many times. Yet I'll be honest—I don't envision a time when I'll be the vocal, uninhibited partner who says, 'Hey baby, let's get it on.' That's just not my style. However, I will continue to send out signals and now I'll even let Stephen know ahead of time which signals mean yes, no, or maybe if you gently get me warmed up."

As a therapist I have heard about similar conversations where the partner who usually doesn't initiate does in fact reveal in these heart-to-heart talks the subtle clues that tonight might be a good night for affection. Some women put on a special piece of clothing or lingerie that signals, "Try me tonight—the stars and the moon are in alignment." Other women and some men say they tend to make especially strong eye contact or they brush up gently against their partner once or twice to signal, "I'm waiting for you to make a move in response."

One woman said, "I don't like to come out and say, 'I'm in the mood!' but it's not hard to read my number one clue that I'm starting to feel a bit amorous. I usually walk up to my partner when he's doing something in the kitchen, the living room, or the bathroom. I gently brush my breasts against his back and wait to see if that gets his attention. What I didn't realize is that my partner has been told no so many times by me on the nights I'm not in the mood that he didn't understand the breasts against the back actually means it's safe again to ask. If we hadn't had this twenty-minute heart-to-heart conversation to clarify the clues, I think I'd still be sending out my signal and he'd still be assuming I'm not interested. Now he knows that when he feels my softness brushing up against his back or he sees me stroking his arm while he's talking, it means the odds are in his favor and he better make a move before the winds change direction."

This question of who initiates and who doesn't may seem inconsequential, but it's not. If year after year there is one partner who gets rejected often and isn't sure what might lead to a yes, then there will eventually be some escalating emotional distance and resentment in the relationship. On the other hand, if you and your partner can give each other a few clues that reveal when you would like to be coaxed into lovemaking (and when you don't want to be coaxed), you will prevent a lot of disappointing moments and hurt feelings. All it takes are a few playful conversations that clarify, "Here's my way of expressing my sensuality without having to blurt it out." Then enjoy the resulting intimacy.

WHAT ABOUT THE AFTERGLOW?

There's one final important choreography issue that has helped hundreds of long-term couples feel more loving, passionate, and satisfied with each other year after year. For many couples, there is a huge difference between a good relationship and a great relationship, depending on how you each handle the afterglow—the quiet, vulnerable moments of connection and bonding that happen (or fail to happen) right after the two of you have reached orgasm or completed your lovemaking.

With your current partner, does that tend to be a moment when the two of you feel extremely close and at peace with the world? Or does your lovemaking frequently end with one of you drifting quickly off to sleep, or one of you taking a phone call, or one of you getting swept away by thoughts about work, money, stressful topics, the kids, sports scores, or domestic chores?

Instead of having one partner longing for closeness while the other partner has gone on to other things, are there alternatives that might help each of you get what you need during the afterglow? Here are a few ideas from my counseling clients. Talk these over with your partner and see which feel right for you and your particular style of post-orgasmic connecting:

* A heterosexual couple told me they like to "spoon" after making love.
* Another heterosexual couple said they usually have only a few minutes after lovemaking until one of them falls asleep, so they maximize these few minutes by making sure they gently kiss each other several times. Sometimes they talk briefly about how grateful they are for the caring, the passion, and the warmth of their lovemaking.
* A lesbian couple told me they feel like the best of teammates at these times.

* A gay male couple told me they prefer silence after love-making, and to drift back into the everyday world slowly without words.

* One heterosexual couple included a male partner who simply couldn't stop himself from falling asleep immediately after climaxing. His partner said she often felt "lonely" and "abandoned" at those moments. So her partner offered to give her something the day after they'd made love, such as a flower, piece of chocolate, romantic note of gratitude, or warm morning kiss, to make sure she knew that he truly did care about their intimate moments.

* Finally, another couple told me they have very active young children who sometimes pound on the locked bedroom door moments after the parents are done making love. According to this couple, "At that moment when we hear the insistent shrieks and fists of our beloved younger child, we look at each other and smile. We're like co-conspirators enjoying the fact that we had some great sex without getting caught. Then we put some clothes on and quickly open the door to hug our insistent child."

Sometimes it takes a bit of creativity and innovation to come up with an afterglow style that works for both partners in a particular situation. Don't judge or attack your partner for needing to sleep after lovemaking or for starting to think about work, food, finances, or the kids. Simply explore with your partner, "What can we do to prolong the closeness and warmth just a few moments more? Can we find a way to give each other reminders of our affection and our appreciation for one another before we move on to our responsibilities?"

As a leaf falling into a pond sends out hundreds of small ripples, so the smallest gestures of caring right after lovemaking can send reminders of your love into your hearts and strengthen your closeness in the hours and days ahead. The beauty of the afterglow of making love is that you can look into each other's eyes for a moment and realize how miraculous it is that you have found someone to love and someone to share life with. Even if you have very stressful lives, those few moments together can become a peaceful sanctuary that revives and renews the two of you.

NAVIGATING THE DAILY TRANSITION FROM WORK MODE TO FULLY PRESENT

Now we come to a crucial issue that on a day-to-day basis can strengthen or deplete your relationship. Imagine that it's been a stressful day—with pressures at work or demands from your children. You and your significant other are having a check-in "How was your day" conversation either on the phone or face to face. All of a sudden one of you starts to tune out because of tiredness or a distracting thought.

The person who's trying to connect begins to suspect that you are barely listening. He or she feels frustrated and says, "Helloooooooooo! Are you even listening?"

Uh-oh, the conversation has turned ugly.

If you were to estimate how often this happens to either you or your partner, would you say it occurs:

a. Once a year?

b. Once a month?

c. Once a week?

d. Almost every day, especially when one of you hasn't had enough sleep and the other partner goes on and on with a complicated story or issue?

Whether you answered a, b, c, or d, there are two important things you need to know. First, you're not a horrible creep for being distracted sometimes when your partner needs you to be fully present. But if you and your partner decide to improve your listening skills even a little, you will dramatically enhance the quality and strength of your relationship. Just by utilizing one or more of the easy-to-follow techniques in this chapter, you will attain a deeper and more satisfying connection to each other, even on stressful days. In fact, this chapter might prevent hundreds of nasty arguments or even save your relationship!

WHAT EXACTLY IS LOUSY LISTENING?

This issue of "Are you really listening?" may seem minor, but in most relationships it is one of the biggest reasons that couples become resentful, drift apart, have affairs, and fall out of love. You might have read the previous sentence and wondered about the words "have affairs." I'm quite serious about this. I have found that, in the majority of cases where men and women wound up hooking up with someone other than their dearly beloved, the most common reason was that the long-term partner wasn't listening anymore and the lover was. I've seen men and women fall out of love and later leave a partner who was a lousy listener even if the lousy listener had big bucks or great looks. So consider yourself lucky to find out the following essential truth about relationships: Even though you might be a great catch, if you're a half-hearted or impatient listener, watch out! My experience with hundreds of couples has told me that your partner might be getting itchy.

Several prominent researchers have shown from extensive scientific studies that the quality of how well the two of you listen and respond to each other in everyday conversations is the glue that holds your relationship together. These research studies have demonstrated that most long-term partnerships can survive just about anything—illness, sexual problems, financial struggles, political clashes, or differing values—but they often get ruined or destroyed by dismissive listening, or by harsh and impatient responses.

DOING YOUR OWN RESEARCH

For a minute or two, imagine that you are an eminent social scientist from Sweden, Nigeria, Japan, or Peru who has been asked to observe a particular two-person relationship to see how the partners listen to each other. As a careful scientist you might spend weeks or months taking notes on what goes on in the relationship. Then you would be asked to present your impartial observations.

If you were this unbiased scientist observing your own relationship for a while, what would you find? Be completely honest. In the past few weeks or months, how often have you or your partner done one or more of the following:

* Looked at a newspaper, book, or magazine while the other person was speaking?

* Tried to have a conversation while the television or the computer was distracting one or both of you?

* Been unable to remember important details of a personal story or a pressing problem that a loved one explained recently?

* Checked your cell phone, your email, your BlackBerry, or another wireless device while a loved one was telling you something he or she considered important?

* Jumped in with advice or a quick fix, when the partner only wanted to be listened to and understood?

* Interrupted or hijacked the conversation by saying, "That reminds me of the time when I . . ."?

* Squashed your partner's enthusiasm or suggestions by saying "No, that'll never work," when there might be a grain of truth or a viable idea worth considering?

* Communicated nonverbal signs of impatience—yawns, frowns, finger tapping, or looking away—while a partner was describing something he or she cares about deeply?

* Said the dreaded words that have launched a thousand fights: "Could you get to the point?" or "Would you just cut to the chase?"?

If you were a scientist, what would your research reveal? From an unbiased scientific assessment, is lousy listening a rare or frequent factor in your relationship? Are the two of you drifting apart because one or both of you get pulled away by frequent distractions? Is some of your tension related to half-hearted listening?

THE LOVING GIFT OF BEING FULLY PRESENT

What would it be like if you and your partner became excellent listeners on a daily basis? For example, think back through the months or years you have known your partner and recall the times when the two of you talked like best friends who truly cared about each other. What did it feel like to have a soul mate who was 100 percent there for you? Wouldn't it be great to have that sense of deep connection again in your conversations?

You may have had moments in your relationship when you both made sure to set aside time each day or each week to catch up on what was happening with each other. Do you remember what that was like, and do you know why you've stopped making your moments together a high priority?

You may have had moments when you felt completely understood and appreciated by each other, when the two of you felt like passionate co-conspirators facing the obstacles and challenges of life together. Did you fall in love because you could appreciate one another's visions and vulnerabilities better than anyone else?

I bring up these questions to help you and your partner remember how amazing it feels when you are absolutely in the current moment connecting with your loved one. Yet to be fully present with the person you love deeply is not easy to accomplish. Not only do we have busy lives and lots to deal with, but we find it risky to open up and be fully known by another human being. On a stressful day when your brain and nervous system get battered and fried, how do you show up and be there 100 percent in the current moment with a partner who might also be exhausted or agitated?

WAYS TO CREATE HEARTFELT LISTENING

No one sets out to be a lousy listener. I doubt that you've ever heard at a wedding or commitment ceremony the partners proclaim in their vows, "I promise to be a mediocre listener to you. I vow to show condescending signs of impatience or say things like 'So what's your point already?' when I come home from work and you're trying to describe the ups and downs of your day." Yet even if you're highly respected as a good listener in your job, you might still need to overcome the tendency to wear your "I've got no listening left" face when you're at home with your long-term partner or your kids.

There are three things you can do to master the art of heartfelt listening, even on a stressful day: the Daily Decompression Exercise, the Twenty-Minute Daily Check-In, and Giving Each Other Three Appreciations.

THE DAILY DECOMPRESSION EXERCISE

It's going to take more than good intentions if you want to be fully present for each other after a stressful day. That's why I recommend a remarkable tool called the Daily Decompression Exercise that I've seen work for hundreds of couples. Instead of going on automatic pilot when you're at home and slipping into impatience or grumpiness, you can use this exercise to manually adjust your focus and breathing at the moment your beloved partner needs you to be fully present. Instead of getting distracted, you can become the exquisite listener that a great partnership requires.

Here's what to do:

Before you try to have a quality conversation with your loved one, take five or ten minutes to "decompress" from the day. You might want to stop a block or two before your street and take five quiet minutes to remind yourself, "I'm not at work any longer. I'm about to enter a different atmosphere where my loved ones are hoping they'll have the good listener this time instead of the cranky, impatient, burned-out basket case they've had to endure too many times."

Or go into the washroom and rinse your hands and face as you say into the mirror, "This is a crucial moment when I'm either going to be a great listener or an impatient jerk. The quality of my relationship depends on whether I show up right now with an open heart or a closed mind."

During your five- or ten-minute decompression, you may also meditate or say a prayer to reconnect with that calm place deep inside yourself. You could say something like, "Please help me open my heart even though my body is tired." Or you could imagine that you're an astronaut or a scuba diver who needs to regain normal breathing now that you're coming back to firm ground after spending time in an alien environment. If you came back suddenly to normal oxygen after a journey to outer space or the ocean floor, you would begin by breathing slowly and calmly as you said to yourself, "I'm entering a completely different world than where I've been the past several hours."

Whatever approach you utilize, make sure you take a moment to feel your body and your mind shifting out of the "get to the point already" tone that might be normal at work but disastrous at home. Breathe deeply as you envision yourself turning back into a loving partner—and a caring and patient parent if you have kids at home.

As you walk up to your front door, stop for a moment to make sure you're ready to approach your loved ones with your most compassionate self. The moment before you say "Hello" or "How are you?" to your loved ones, take a deep breath and remind yourself, "The person I'm about to talk to is more important than any client, customer, boss, colleague, or phone caller I've spoken to today. I better show up fully available for this next conversation because nothing else is as important as these precious moments together." You might even want to put these few sentences on a note card that you keep in your wallet in case you need to read them to yourself after an especially stressful day.

Even if your partner or your kids start right in saying something you've heard before, remind yourself that you can still be a calm and patient listener. As your partner begins to speak, if you notice that your impatience, irritability, or desire to interrupt is welling up, be sure to catch yourself and say silently, "Don't be a jerk. Don't be the lousy listener who can ruin a good relationship. Right now I'm definitely tired, but I'm still capable of listening with a completely open heart. This is the moment to prove whether I'm a great partner or a cranky burden for my loved ones."

Please don't underestimate the importance of this decompression portion of your day. What you say to yourself to unhook from your stressed-out mood is up to you. I've listed here a few possibilities, but feel free to change these statements into your own words. The key is to find a way to decompress so you won't stir up a fight or disappoint those who look forward to seeing you when you come home. Because if you talk to your partner or your kids the way you talk to someone you are disciplining at work, your loved ones will be thinking to themselves, "Oh, great, here we go again. The agitated commander in chief is home again and we're all supposed to take orders. Get me outta here!"

"It's Not like at Work Where People Know They've Got Two Minutes or Less to Wrap It Up"

Vanessa's case is a good illustration of how powerful this decompression technique can be for improving the way you communicate with your loved ones after a stressful day. Vanessa is a highly respected, well-liked, mid-level manager at a large company. Her colleagues and her boss are often amazed at how well she holds it together day after day, even when an irate employee or an aggressive customer is screaming in her face or making life difficult.

Yet when Vanessa comes home to be with her handsome and talented actor boyfriend, Richie, and his two young children from a previous relationship, she describes how "I just don't have any more patience or listening ability left. Richie starts telling me about his frustrations in looking for a new job and I feel like cutting him off after ten seconds to give him advice. Or I hear how he handled a situation with one of the kids and I can't listen patiently. I find myself interrupting him and correcting him, which rubs Richie the wrong way because he hates to be told what to do."

According to Vanessa, "Not only is it hard to listen when Richie tells me about his day, but the kids want me to get down on the floor and play Legos or Playmobil with them, even though I've got nothing left to give. Or they go on and on with stories. It's not like at work where people know they've got two minutes or less to wrap it up. I sometimes feel like an outsider in my own home because Richie and the kids are usually in the mood for hanging out and just being together as a family. But I'm worn out from a long day and all I want to do is handle a few details and then numb out for the rest of the evening."

Like many people who are great listeners during the day but who find themselves impatient or short-tempered with their loved ones, Vanessa has a problem. She admits, "I love Richie and the kids a lot, so it really hurt when he told me last week, 'I was extremely attracted to you, Vanessa, in the beginning because you were kind to me and to my kids. But living with you these past three years has shown me a different side of you. You're so quick to interrupt and give advice to the ones you love and you cut us a lot less slack than the people at work who think you're an angel.'"

In couples counseling with Vanessa and Richie, we worked on several issues. First, we explored what Richie could do to improve his chances for finding work. Then we discussed how to bring Richie's style of parenting closer in line with Vanessa's style.

In addition, I asked Vanessa if she would be willing to try the decompression exercise to help her bring home the good listening skills she uses at work. At first she was skeptical and said, "I feel like I gave at the office and there ain't nothing left by the time I get home." But when she finally tried the decompression exercise, she found a renewed sense of inner strength and an ability to listen. As she described a few weeks later, "I knew I didn't want to lose Richie or be cut off from the kids. So I decided to take five or ten minutes each day before entering the house to see if it might make a difference. Just to breathe deeply, say a prayer, and ask God for a little more strength and endurance to be able to come through for the people I love. I worried that I might have nothing left to give, but those five or ten minutes of gentle unwinding helped me begin to make a successful shift from the tensions of work to the different kind of intensity in my home life."

Vanessa explained, "I reminded myself each night that this was a crucial moment of shifting from my workplace, where the rules of efficiency operate, to my home life, where Richie and the children don't give a hoot about efficiency. After a week or two of decompressing on the way home each night, I probably was a lot more pleasant to be around."

However, Vanessa admitted, "Sometimes I still come home

with so much unfinished junk in my head from work. On those nights I've found I definitely need to pull out the note card from my wallet and say to myself before I walk in the front door, 'The loved ones I'm about to talk to are more important than any client, customer, boss, colleague, or phone caller I've spoken to today. They're in my heart and I better show up fully available for these next few conversations because nothing else is as important as these moments together.' If I happen to forget to look at the note card or say those words, I tend to slip back into feeling impatient or interrupting. It's one day at a time because the tensions from work are huge and they're always there, ready to burst out. I wish it were easy or automatic, but it's not. Especially after certain high-pressure days, when everyone wants something from me at work, I absolutely need these tools in order to stay on track."

While Richie and Vanessa still had work to do in couples counseling on how to successfully co-parent two demanding children, their listening and their closeness improved dramatically over the next few weeks and months. According to Richie, "I can't deny the fact that I'd started to fall out of love with Vanessa. I even fantasized about what life would be like with someone who was a little less stressed and a lot easier to talk to at night. Yet that was not a road I was ready to go down. I do care about Vanessa, and lately when we talk each night, the connection is so pure and so deep. It's like when we met four years ago and first fell in love. Both of us still have stressful lives with a lot of daily pressures, but at least our relationship is as strong as it's ever been."

THE TWENTY-MINUTE DAILY CHECK-IN

Have you ever tried to listen to and relate to your partner but he or she simply would not stop talking? It's not easy to stay fully alert if your loved one is going on and on for an hour or two in a monologue. Or the problem might be that your partner is the strong, silent type, which is another way of saying, "This person simply will not talk about his or her inner life." If you ask, "What's new?" the answer is likely to be "Nothing." If you ask, "How are you?" the answer is usually "Fine." If you ask, "Is there anything you want to tell me about your day?" the answer is probably "Not really." Kinda makes you want to scream, doesn't it?

That's why I recommend some specific invitational phrases for starting your "How was your day?" check-in conversation. One that works for the majority of hard-working and emotionally drained couples is, "I want to hear what's going on with you. Let's take twenty minutes—ten minutes for each of us. Do you want to go first or second?"

Knowing that you're each going to get your own ten minutes to speak allows you to relax and not interrupt your partner's ten minutes. Knowing that your partner is only going to talk for ten minutes also gives you a good reason to listen intently when he or she speaks. Even when you're tired or stressed, you probably still have ten minutes of heartfelt listening left in you.

If you've never tried this positive and sensible daily check-in technique, please give it a try. You will be amazed at how much better the two of you will listen and share your inner lives when you each know you'll be having an uninterrupted ten minutes to be heard by your loved one.

"The Problem with Us Is That My Partner Loves to Talk and Talk and Talk"

Here's one example of how the twenty-minute daily check-in technique can dramatically improve the quality of your relationship. Evan and Clay entered couples counseling a year ago because they are a hard-working, two-career couple who never have time any more to talk like best friends, and it's causing them to feel distant from each other. Evan explained during their first session, "I'm getting worried that Clay is having great conversations each day at work and over drinks with his colleagues, but by the time he comes home he's got nothing left. Even if I encourage him and say, 'How was your day?' or 'What's on your mind lately?,' he gives me this blank stare and says, 'It's just the same old, same old. Nothing much to tell.'"

Clay described the situation differently: "The problem with us is that Evan loves to talk and talk and talk. He'll give me long explanations of the office politics at work, as well as full details about his creative ideas and his struggles with his crazy family. I'm more of an old-fashioned guy who doesn't have much to say unless I'm absolutely in the right mood to spill my guts. You ask me 'How are you?' and I'll say 'Fine,' which essentially means 'Back off . . . I don't feel like rehashing the frustrations of my day right now.' Especially after a long, stressful nine hours at work, I don't want Evan pressuring me to open up and talk. But Evan would love to dish every night, and he's frustrated that I'd rather play a video game or read a good book to unwind."

Like many couples in which one partner is a talker and the other is a silent type, Evan and Clay were starting to drift apart. Evan was concerned because "we've been together for six years, but we're starting to become strangers. I don't even know the names of the people Clay has hired or fired in the past six months. Entire weeks go by and we're like two ships passing in the night, saying hi to each other but not really talking."

When I first recommended the twenty-minute daily check-in technique to Evan and Clay, they were both a bit hesitant. Evan the talker said, "I only get ten minutes?" Clay the quieter one said, "How am I gonna fill up all that time? I don't need to be saying something profound for the entire ten minutes, do I?"

Yet as I've found with hundreds of other couples, the comforting structure and reliability of the twenty-minute daily check-in technique began to strengthen their relationship after only a few days of trying it. Evan found, "I've always wanted to have Clay truly be there and listen with an open heart. I've noticed that Clay is much more relaxed and fully listening now that he knows I'm *only* going to talk for ten minutes or so. His yawns, his sense of irritation, and his tuning out are gone. It actually feels like a quality relationship again."

Clay said, "I wasn't sure at first that I'd want to talk for an entire ten minutes each night. But I discovered after a few tries that it's a rather enjoyable amount of time. I decided to let Evan know a few things about what's on my mind and what really matters to me. And Evan is jazzed about all this because we're finally able to talk and check in each night, instead of going into our separate worlds in different parts of the house."

One final note about the twenty-minute daily check-in: In some cases, you and your partner might want to design an "exception" to the twenty-minute structure. On some nights one of you might want helpful input or advice at the end of your ten minutes. Or you might have something very complex or upsetting to discuss and you know in advance it will take fifteen or twenty minutes to give it justice. On those nights the two of you can revise the structure to whatever suits you, as long as you make sure both of you will get an uninterrupted turn to speak. The goal is to help both of you escape from work pressures and fully connect with each other and catch up on your inner lives. You might need to experiment with various amounts of time or routines in order to make it happen consistently throughout your busy week.

GIVING EACH OTHER THREE APPRECIATIONS

At the end of a stressful day, what people want most is not to be criticized or judged, but rather to be appreciated and honored for their hard work and efforts. That's why it is important for you and your partner to each say what the other one has done well lately. This may sound mushy or overly sentimental to some people, but it's an incredibly powerful way to make the shift from stress mode to fully present mode when you are talking to your loved one. Here's how it works:

Come up with three things that are true and positive. At least once a week, during your evening meal or your twenty-minute check-in, or in bed before switching off the light, spend a few minutes saying to each other, "Three things I appreciate about you lately are _____, _____, and _____." The three appreciations may be large or small, obvious or subtle. They may be personal things like "I've always loved your eyes" or "I'm glad you've got such a strong sense of integrity." They may be acknowledgments of action, such as "I appreciate that you had the guts to stand up to my older brother last week when he was trashing me at the family dinner" or "I appreciate that you rinsed and stacked the dishes this morning before you went to work." Or a mention of small gestures like "I appreciate that you left me a voice mail message saying you and the kids had gotten home safely in the rainstorm." Or something quick and yet profound, such as "I'm glad you work as hard as you do to keep us afloat."

Rather than exaggerating, being phony, or talking in a patronizing voice, the three appreciations at the end of a stressful day should be true and solid. They should be genuine and sincere. If you are able to notice and verbalize what's going right during the most difficult days, you will have a powerful method for snapping out of the irritability that you feel in your high-pressure life. With your three appreciations, you are essentially saying to your partner, "We're good teammates. We're definitely in this together. We're moving the ball forward one day at a time. We can count on each other—not to be perfect, but to be good to each other."

Studies show that appreciations build up a bank of goodwill

that acts as a buffer for two people during the down times in daily life. If you and your partner only talk about what's going wrong or what's still undone, you will find yourselves increasingly stressed and irritated with each other. On the other hand, if you take turns giving each other three or more appreciations on a stressful day, you will find that you have far more resilience and attention for dealing with the struggles in your careers and personal lives.

Now here's an interesting fact about the Three Appreciations technique: Research shows that the vast majority of people find it easier to come up with criticisms and things that irritate them about their partner than to come up with appreciations or things that are going well. In 1927 there was a fascinating scientific study by psychologist Bluma Zeigarnik in which she asked people to look at a circle that was seven-eighths complete. She found that the vast majority of people focused on the one-eighth of the circle that was missing. From this and other studies, Zeigarnik and her team of cognitive researchers came up with a theory called the Zeigarnik Effect, namely that our brains are geared toward trying to resolve what isn't complete, so we are less likely to spend time noticing what has gone right or what is already complete. It's as though our brains are designed by God, nature, or genetics to be problem-seeking missiles that look for unresolved problems while ignoring or taking for granted things that are running smoothly or already completed.

So if you or your partner tend to fixate on how the other person loads the dishwasher "incorrectly," fails to close the tooth-paste tube, or leaves clothes on the floor next to the bed, it simply means you've each got a good problem-seeking brain. According to the Zeigarnik Effect, the majority of people have problem-seeking brains; thus, we have to consciously refocus our attention on those qualities or actions that are positive and running smoothly, or we won't notice them at all.

That's why an exercise such as the Three Appreciations is crucial if you want to have a healthy and enjoyable relationship. Otherwise you will slip back into seeing only what's problematic or incomplete in your relationship. By taking a few minutes once or twice a week to let your partner know that you have been listening and appreciating his or her good qualities and caring efforts, you can make a huge difference in the way the two of you feel about each other and your relationship. Instead of having a partner who is your harshest critic or toughest person to satisfy, you might begin to enjoy life with someone who not only points out the things you need to work on but also tells you frequently, "I appreciate who you are and what you do," or who says in words and actions, "I'm grateful for your strengths and your essential goodness. I'm glad we're on this journey together."

"I Don't Need to Stroke Someone's Ego. That's Just Not Who I Am."

While most of the couples I've counseled have enjoyed and quickly learned how to benefit from the Three Appreciations exercise, one particular couple included a partner who won the award for the Human Being Least Likely to Give a Compliment.

Burt is a competent accountant who has been married to Gwen, a clothing designer, for seventeen years. When they first came in for counseling, Gwen said, "My husband Burt is highly regarded at work as a no-nonsense professional. But at home he's sometimes quite critical and hard to please. I often feel like no matter what I do to make his life easier, he finds something to pick at."

Burt rolled his eyes as she said that. Then he commented, "She always paints it like I'm some sort of ogre. My wife is very insecure and she needs everyone to tell her how great she is. Well, I'm not a phony and I don't butter people up. I love Gwen—always have and always will. But I don't need to stroke someone's ego. That's just not who I am."

Then Burt went on to explain, "Where I work there are the sales and marketing types who always give people compliments in order to talk them into something. Then there are the accountants, like me, who just tell people the unvarnished truth. Gwen knows I'm not a bullshitter. So when I come home from work and see something that's clearly not right around the house, I just tell her. No baloney. No dishonesty. Is that so terrible?"

At first I was unable to get Burt to consider the benefits of lightening up a bit on his nightly unvarnished truth telling, which was causing his wife and two teenage daughters to pull away from him. Burt told me he was convinced that "honesty is the best policy," and he believed strongly that all compliments and appreciations were a "phony game to pull the wool over someone's eyes."

While I agree with Burt that honesty is a good thing, sometimes too much "unvarnished truth" can spell trouble if people bombard their loved ones with a litany of complaints—especially if there is little or no time given to pointing out what they're doing right. So I decided to ask Burt to put his accountant skills to work in analyzing the listening and communication patterns he and Gwen use. Near the end of the first counseling session, I gave Burt the same homework assignment I've given many people who have excellent problem-seeking brains. I told Burt, "During the next seven days, jot down a thorough accounting of each thing your wife is doing well and each thing she isn't doing quite the way you'd like it done. Then bring in the debits and credits list so we can see what it looks like from your point of view. Sound fair?"

Burt smiled. "Sounds easy. All you want me to do is keep a seven-day ledger of things I notice about my wife. I'll have it for you next week. No problem."

A week later, Burt came in with an extensive list of debits and credits. It was immediately apparent, however, that the list was highly out of balance. On the debits side, Burt had listed seventy-two times that Gwen had done something he didn't like. On the credits side, there were only four entries.

I said to Burt, "You did a good job of collecting data. But it sure looks lopsided, doesn't it?"

Burt said, "Sure does, but I love her anyway."

I replied to Burt, "I hope you won't get offended by this, but I'm willing to bet that your method for noticing what Gwen is doing well and what she isn't doing well might not be 100 percent accurate."

Burt looked surprised. No one had ever suggested that his methods might be inaccurate. So I told Burt about the Zeigarnik research that shows how the brain over-notices the unresolved problems and under-focuses on things that are complete or going well. He was interested in this issue of accuracy, so I asked, "What if there were some credits—some things that Gwen is doing right—that you didn't notice or that you failed to put down on the accounting ledger? What if, for some reason, your particular talent is finding debits, but you're not as attuned to finding credits?"

I sensed that Burt was upset with my questioning his accuracy. After all, he's got more than twenty years of experience as an accountant, and I'm just a touchy-feely shrink. But to Burt's credit, he hung in there, and near the end of the session we came up with a second homework assignment. I said, "This time see if you can override the part of your brain that seeks to identify things that aren't going well, and instead write down a positive statement when Gwen does something right. Are you willing to do that?"

Burt replied, "You bet I'm willing. I certainly don't want this to be inaccurate. That's not my style."

A week later he came in with a ledger that had "only" forty criticisms and about thirty compliments. I said, "Good job. It's getting closer to a balanced ledger."

By the fourth week his ledger was 50/50. I gave him a high five and said, "Way to go, Burt. Now you're really paying attention!"

During that same counseling session, I asked Burt and Gwen to start trying the Three Appreciations exercise once or twice a week to see if it felt honest and accurate to them, or if it felt forced and phony. To help Burt get on board, I explained that the purpose of the Three Appreciations exercise is not to butter up your partner or be a sales and marketing type. The purpose is to outsmart the part of our brain that only notices or remembers what's going wrong. Since we've all got this somewhat inaccurate way of seeing things—a problem-obsessed, fault-seeking focus—we've all got to take responsibility for being more accurate and decent in the way we talk to our loved ones. The Three Appreciations technique is the quickest way to focus your brain on what most people overlook about their long-time partner and their kids—the daily efforts, the simple gestures of love and kindness, and the good qualities that you've started to take for granted.

I'm happy to report that Burt and Gwen began to give each other a few verbal acknowledgments each week. According to Gwen, "I had doubts about whether Burt would ever go along with something so positive. But he's actually quite good at it. Once or twice a week I hear a few words of warm acknowledgment from my no-nonsense husband. And when Burt says he likes something about the way I look or the way I'm doing things, I know for certain it's got to be the truth because God knows, Burt doesn't offer any phony butter-'em-up stroking."

During their final counseling session a few weeks later, Burt told me something interesting: "I still feel a little bit uncomfortable sometimes when I'm saying all this flattering stuff to my wife. Not that I'm worried she might get a big head or become egotistical. Gwen is still a fairly humble and down-to-earth person. But giving a few appreciations is just not how I was raised, and I don't really understand why people need so much praise in order to feel okay about themselves. I wish it weren't necessary, yet I do want to be accurate and Gwen definitely loves this stuff. So I figure, what's the harm in being a little bit positive? It's cheaper than buying a diamond necklace, I'll tell you that."

One final word about the Three Appreciations method: If you or your partner feel uncomfortable about the formality of listing exactly three good things about each other once or twice a week, feel free to adjust the routine to whatever suits your style. You can say them at more spontaneous and less-structured times. Or you can switch between offering two or four or even six appreciations weekly. Or you can try your own words and your own style for letting your partner know, "I've been paying attention and I do admire all the things that you're doing to make our lives better."

If someone like Burt can notice and verbalize three appreciations to help improve his relationship, I'm willing to bet that you and your partner can do it, too. The worst that may happen is that the positive and warm feelings generated by these Three Appreciations might seem unfamiliar and unusual, especially if you grew up in a household or a culture where criticism and put-downs were more common. Instead of hurting a loved one with too many criticisms and sarcastic comebacks, you will be reminding each other on a frequent basis why the two of you are still in love.

MAKING DOMESTIC TEAMWORK
MORE "TEAM" AND LESS "WORK"

Let me clue you in to a secret. In the world of couples therapy, the topics of sex and communication get most of the attention. But on a daily basis, a large percentage of the irritations and arguments in nearly every relationship occur because of clashes regarding domestic chores.

Have you ever gotten irritated with your partner because he or she deals with household responsibilities differently than you do? Maybe one of you likes things neat and orderly, while the other person is oblivious about cleaning up. Or it might be that one of you is comfortable with children and adept at child care and setting limits with your kids, while the other partner is far less involved. Or maybe one of you tends to do too many of the household chores and resents the imbalance. Or possibly one of you has fallen behind on some important fix-it or home improvement projects while the other partner is frustrated about the delay.

This chapter will *not* be about blame or name-calling (even if you're tempted to say, "You obsessive neat freak" or "You lazy slob"). Rather, I will be offering specific, positive ways for building a much stronger sense of teamwork, fun, and satisfaction in your daily life together. Think of this step as a magic bullet to improving your relationship now.

BUILDING A "TEAM" MENTALITY

Over the years, I've learned from counseling clients and close friends some creative ways of resolving the domestic teamwork issues that flare up in otherwise good relationships. As you examine each of the following ways of improving your home life, see which approaches you're already doing with your partner and which new approaches might be worth a try. Feel free to disagree with any of the suggestions or to say "Not a chance" to an unusual alternative that seems too outrageous for you or your partner. But try at least one or two of these highly effective methods to see if they can resolve the power struggles and irritations that have shown up in your relationship regarding domestic tasks. Because if you and your partner can build a solid team mentality toward these tasks to help avoid the adversarial moments that couples face when they clash about household chores, your fragile relationship has a far better chance of surviving—and, believe me, thriving.

HOUSEHOLD TEAMWORK AS A WEEKLY GAME

Let's go right to one of the more unusual ideas that has worked successfully for hundreds of couples. I call it the Weekly Teamwork Contest, and you and your partner can co-design it to fit your own styles.

You might be skeptical at first about whether it's possible to think of kitchen chores, changing diapers, home repairs, or dusting as pleasurable activities. Most couples talk about their household responsibilities with the same enthusiasm that they have for a proctology appointment or a visit to the Department of Motor Vehicles. But what if you turned these chores into a pleasurable weekly game that caused both partners to be excited and enthusiastic about doing well? Here's how it works.

At a prearranged time each week (maybe Wednesday night or Friday morning or Sunday night), take fifteen minutes with your partner to list seven to ten household tasks that need to be done over the next week. Then assign a small but attractive prize that will be awarded to the person who does each unpopular task. The more of these less-than-exciting tasks a person does, the more prizes he or she receives each week. Write the list of tasks on a small note card, along with the promised prizes. Then keep the note card in your purse or wallet for handy reference.

The prize can be anything that you and your partner might enjoy working hard to receive. For instance, some couples offer each other a five-dollar or twenty-dollar "I can spend it any way I want to" cash prize for doing a weekly task. Or a piece of chocolate. Or an ice cream sandwich. Or breakfast in bed. Or a sexual favor. Or a neck massage. Or a foot massage. Or control of the TV remote for a few days. For long and difficult projects, a prize may be awarded for each segment of the project that gets completed during that week.

At the end of the week, when you sit down to plan the next

week's tasks, you either award the prize or agree on a time to do so. There's no failure or criticism, just prizes for tasks completed, while the unfinished tasks get placed on the next week's list. The purpose of this weekly teamwork contest is to inspire the two of you to come up with enjoyable prizes and strong motivations for each partner to pitch in and help with burdensome tasks.

In some relationships where there has been an imbalance between the partner who claims to be too busy to do very many of the household tasks and the partner who usually does too many of the household tasks, this prize system can help even things out. The partner who tends to do more can quickly begin to build up a nest egg of "I can spend it any way I want to" funds, or enjoy the other prizes. Meanwhile, the partner who usually does less will begin to wonder, "Why am I saying no to these attractive prizes? Maybe I ought to do a few more tasks each week and share in the spoils."

"Can the Prize Be *Anything*?"

One outrageous example of how this Weekly Teamwork Contest works for many creative couples involves Danielle and Jordan. They've been together for almost six years and they both work hard at highly stressful jobs—with very little energy left over for domestic chores. This used to cause a lot of arguments because Jordan likes things neat and orderly, while Danielle tends to be casual and unconcerned about cleanliness. So Jordan found himself sometimes resenting Danielle and often criticizing her about her messiness because he cleaned up after her month after month. Then they came in for counseling and I told them about the Weekly Teamwork Contest.

As soon as I mentioned the possibility of unique and individualized prizes, Danielle asked, "Can the prize be *anything?*" I said, "Anything that doesn't offend either one of you and that your budget can afford."

So Danielle asked Jordan, "Would you be offended if I asked you to contribute some oral sex to the prize category?" Jordan looked a little embarrassed and explained, "I'm not 100 percent comfortable with giving oral sex, but Danielle loves it. I guess if that's what she wants for making things more balanced in terms of domestic teamwork, I'm okay with that."

Danielle added, "Since we're on that topic, I should clarify that I'm hoping for some of your highly affectionate, very involved oral sex as the prize—not the 'let's get it over with' kind." Jordan smiled a mischievous grin and said, "I think that's a legitimate request."

From that day forward, Danielle and Jordan had a lot of fun co-designing prizes for their weekly chores. For the first time since they had begun living together, their stressful lives and their differing ideas about tidiness were no longer a source of conflict. Jordan loved the fact that their mutual participation in keeping their home clean was now much closer to 50/50. At the same time, Danielle reported she was quite happy with the excellent quality of her weekly prize (and in many cases it was plural: prizes).

Whether the prize is a sexual treat, twenty dollars, or an ice cream dessert, these contests often make the most routine chores fun and playful. The weekly prizes might seem like bribes, but most couples find them enjoyable treats that bring playfulness and co-operation to a potentially stressful area of life. Rather than arguing about who does more or who is being treated unfairly, couples find that the Weekly Teamwork Contest simply motivates both partners to create fun prizes and enjoy the chores the two of them select.

One female client said to me, "I used to resent that my husband just assumed I would do 70 percent or 80 percent of the child care—the early morning wake-ups, the errand-running, the food preparation, and the late-night cleanup. But ever since we turned this into a weekly game, he's been willing to volunteer for more of the chores, and he's also been more reliable on some of the fix-up projects he'd been stalling on for months. For the first time, he's been doing his fair share of waking up the kids because it means he gets to control the TV remote clicker for a week or go out for his favorite frozen yogurt treats. Now, at the end of the week when I collect several prizes and he collects several prizes, we both feel great about the teamwork and cooperation we've created."

HOUSEHOLD TEAMWORK AS AN ACT OF REBELLION

For some couples, sharing domestic chores and child care is not a game but an important and serious issue of fairness and respect. Especially if you grew up in a family where you saw one parent constantly refuse to do his or her fair share, it might be frustrating to see a similar imbalance occur in your own adult relationship. Or if you suffered emotionally in a previous relationship with someone who was critical about domestic chores or unwilling to share tasks, you might feel strongly about avoiding similar imbalances in your current relationship. If you've had such an experience, or seen it happen to someone else, you know that the bitter feelings can tear away at even a good relationship.

So for some couples, setting up a partnership in which child care and domestic chores are shared equitably (or at least more equitably) is a profound way to rebel against the unfairness of the past. It's a way to express personal opposition to the hurtful assumptions of prior generations and declare with your current partner, "This is *our* household and *we* get to make the new rules. We get to design a partnership with a sense of fairness and mutual respect that prior generations couldn't imagine."

"Congratulations, You Have Officially Become Your Father!"

Mario is a thirty-four-year-old engineer, originally from New York. He grew up in a household where his highly educated mother was often yelled at by his less-educated but very demanding father, who forced Mario's mom to do nearly all of the domestic chores, child care, and errand-running. Mario remembers as a teenager watching his father come home at night in a bad mood. Most nights he would hear his father criticize his mother because a chore hadn't been done or a shirt hadn't been pressed properly, and tell her that she wasn't doing enough. As Mario listened to his parents' heated arguments about household chores and child-care issues, he recalls saying to himself, "My father is a self-centered prick who thinks everyone should cater to his whims." Mario promised himself silently, "I will never treat anyone like that. My mother deserves to be talked to with respect for all that she does."

Flash forward nineteen years. Mario is married and has a young child. He admits, "When my wife Julianne and I moved in together three years ago, I kinda resented that she would ask me to clean up around the house, change lightbulbs, or fix screen doors and toilets that were broken. After a hard day at work, I didn't even want to think about household responsibilities. I just wanted to kick back with a beer and watch sports on television like I did when I was single."

Mario continues, "Then a year ago we had our first child and I'll be honest—I still didn't want to do very much around the house. One night I was watching an important basketball game on television and Julianne called out to me from the next room, 'Mario, look quickly! Your baby girl is walking on her own! Please, Mario. Look at her!'

"Apparently my daughter had taken her very first steps. But at that moment my eyes were glued to the TV because the Knicks were down by two points and they were going for a three-point shot at the buzzer. This hot-dog rookie got the ball and decided that he was gonna be a hero. But he missed the shot. I kicked over a tray with chips and beer on it as I waited to see the final shot one more time on the replay. The idiot should have passed, but instead he put up an air ball that cost us the game. I was furious.

"There were tears in Julianne's eyes as she stood there watching me totally immersed in the damn basketball game. Then she said, 'Mario, congratulations. You have officially become your father!'"

That was the start of a screaming match between Mario and Julianne. He called her a bitch. She called him a selfish bastard. She told him she was sad for him because he cared more about sports on television than he cared about his wife and daughter. Mario stormed out and it took him several hours to cool down enough to come back into the house.

Under orders from Julianne—"Either you call a therapist or I'm calling a lawyer"—Mario came in for counseling the next week. At first he sounded like a victim, saying that he'd been quite happy being single and wondered why Julianne was always so irritated with him. Like many first-time clients in therapy, he was trying to convince me how innocent he was and how wrong everyone else was.

But I said, "I know you were sent here under pressure. That's okay. In fact, most men first attend counseling under pressure. For the record, I was also sent to counseling under pressure many years ago, so we're in the same boat. But as long as you're here, is there anything about yourself that you want to work on and maybe improve so you don't wind up paying for an expensive divorce?"

Surprised by the directness of my comments, Mario smiled and admitted, "That fight the other night with my wife really got to me. I'm hoping that was as bad as it's gonna get."

I asked him gently, "What do you mean, 'as bad as it's gonna get'?"

Mario took a deep breath and said, "I don't want my marriage to be a constant power struggle. I want it to be much better than it's been lately. I finally saw during that moment when my daughter was taking her first steps and my wife was begging me to pay

119

attention—I saw that I was being the same kind of 'cater-to-me' jerk that my father had been. I swear to you, I don't want to let that happen."

During his sessions, Mario began to reexamine the promise he had made to himself nineteen years ago not to become like his father. We also explored the kind of husband and father he did want to be. As a result, Mario began to make some changes. He started to volunteer to help out around the house, even though it was difficult for him. In fact, he was quite uncomfortable at first spending time alone with his daughter, and a bit clumsy initially at communicating with her. In the past, when his daughter had cried or become fussy, Mario had just handed her back to her mother. Now he was getting down on the floor and playing with her and trying to soothe her when she was hungry, tired, or upset.

Mario still watched sports on television occasionally, but he was more likely to clean up his messes and do more of the household chores. His marriage got stronger as a result, although Mario admitted, "There's still a part of me that is a slacker, a part of me that wants to kick back at the end of a hard day at work and let everyone cater to my needs. But the changes I'm making are more important than anything I've ever done in my life. Building a balanced and healthy partnership with my wife Julianne means I'm gonna have to keep learning new stuff and growing in ways that I never saw my dad learn or grow. I could easily go back to my old ways, but I'm committed now to making sure my wife and my daughter don't end up resenting me the way I've always resented my old man."

HOUSEHOLD TEAMWORK AS A SPIRITUAL ACT

In couples where one or both partners are spiritual or religious, there is another unconventional way of looking at the issues of household chores and child-care responsibilities. In most spiritual traditions there is the concept of stewardship, which means lovingly taking care of something precious and fragile—something entrusted to you for a higher purpose. In some Catholic and Protestant congregations, priests and ministers talk about being a steward in life and taking good care of the gifts God has given you. In Hebrew, the word is *shomeir:* a protector and keeper of God's creations. In Jewish teachings, a shomeir is the person who protects the holiness and sacredness of something important, such as the Sabbath, the holidays, the congregation's activities, or the peacefulness of home life.

In several Eastern religions, "karma yoga" involves viewing each mundane task of daily work or domestic effort as a way to become mindful of your oneness with the Infinite. Similarly, in Native American cultures, taking good care of your living space is important because it is a sacred gift that connects you to all the elements of nature and the world.

Whatever religious or spiritual tradition you come from, or even if you are currently not part of a spiritual tradition, you might find it useful to view each household task as a kind of stewardship. Where you live is entrusted to you by God or Spirit or life as a precious and fragile place that you need to care for if you want it to enable you and your loved ones to grow, relax, be secure, and stay connected.

On a financial level, you might own or rent your home or apartment, and you might be the one who pays the mortgage or the rent. But from a spiritual perspective, the bricks, wood, earth, sunshine, breezes, shade, and precious individuals that are part of your home come originally from a higher Source. Looked at from this perspective, you don't really "own" the beauty, warmth, solidness, and nurturing in your home, but you have responsibility for taking good care of it.

So here's the spiritual question for you and your partner: What would your daily attitude and actions be if the two of you began to view your household teamwork as an opportunity to be stewards of a sacred space, your home? If you are appreciative of what life or God or Spirit has given you, then you will probably want to take good care of it. I'm not talking about perfection or obsessive cleanliness here. I'm just talking about an attitude of gratitude that enables you and your partner to look at your household tasks and child-care responsibilities as precious gifts or links in a chain of creation.

Instead of viewing each diaper change, lightbulb replacement, and load of laundry as an unwelcome burden, you might begin to feel humble and grateful when you perform these tasks, and to interpret tickling an infant's belly during a diaper change as an act of holiness. You're taking good care of one of God's creations or life's miracles. Or when you're folding and putting away a load of freshly cleaned laundry, you're not just doing a "chore," but you're making it possible for warmth, connection, and feelings of self-worth to occur for those that you love.

Each of us gets to choose how we view our household tasks. I remember that when I would get up in the middle of the night to change my son's diaper, I occasionally saw it as a burden and had an attitude of resentment. As a result, the diaper-changing ritual felt frustrating and stressful. But when I successfully shifted to a spiritual perspective and reminded myself that my son was truly a miracle in my life, I felt quite differently about cleaning up after him. When I looked at this three A.M. activity as a way to connect with my beloved son and to protect and care for an important gift, it began to feel like a holy act. Yes, I was tired and disoriented at three A.M. But it was a rare and wonderful chance to listen to the beautiful silence of the night and the remarkable sound of my son's breathing. When your adorable child is sleeping innocently in front of you, you can almost sense his or her pure soul there before your eyes.

"I Never Imagined We'd Break Up over Messiness"

A practical example of how spiritual stewardship can improve a relationship comes from Alice and Georgina, a couple I counseled for almost a year. When Alice and Georgina first met at a friend's dinner party, they immediately felt a strong attraction. Their first few months of dating were extremely pleasurable for both of them. But when they decided to live together, a serious problem arose.

Alice, who works for a prominent furniture design firm, is a highly organized, meticulous person when it comes to interior design, home remodeling, and keeping things neat and orderly. On the other hand, Georgina, a songwriter and novelist, is far less interested in what their home looks like; she cares about having a casual and welcoming environment for their two cats and their close friends who visit often.

Alice will tell you that she thinks dusting, cleaning, and home improvements should be a top priority for any couple. But if you ask Georgina, she'll admit she couldn't care less about dusting, cleaning, or home improvements—except she does tend to put all the piles of saved newspapers, unwashed laundry, and unopened mail in a corner of the back bedroom when certain "opinionated" guests visit.

During the first few years that they lived together, Alice was trying hard to be open-minded and not too critical of Georgina. As Alice admitted, "I never imagined we'd break up over messiness."

But three years into their relationship, Alice and Georgina adopted an active and challenging infant named Jenna. Now the battle over messiness intensified. According to Alice, "Prior to Jenna coming into our life, I tried with all my might not to take it personally that Georgina wouldn't keep a clean home just for my benefit. But with Jenna crawling around on the floor and climbing all over the place, I get very upset and quite judgmental when Georgina is unwilling to keep things as clean and orderly as I believe they need to be now that we've got a child."

In counseling, Georgina offered a different perspective. "It's true I'm somewhat oblivious to household chores. I respect that Alice has an incredible visual capacity, which makes her a great designer but also causes her to see dirt and chaos where I see piles of interesting material and boxes of items that aren't hurting anyone.

Yet I'm worried that if Alice and I don't stop arguing and resenting each other over messiness, we're going to create an unhealthy environment for Jenna or break up."

Near the end of their first counseling session, I found out something from Georgina that I thought might help; namely, that both Alice and Georgina have a strong sense of spirituality. For Alice, that includes her long-time involvement in a congregation that has accepted and welcomed her sexual orientation and her relationship with Georgina. For Georgina, who has shied away from organized religion because her family members and their congregational leaders vehemently disapprove of her sexual orientation, spirituality is a more private and personal experience. According to Georgina, "Even though it's been years since I've felt comfortable in a formal religious setting, I still have a deep connection to prayer and an appreciation of the mysterious wonders and holy moments of life."

I asked Alice and Georgina if they'd be willing to explore the concept of spiritual stewardship now that they were sharing a home and raising a child together. As a homework assignment, I asked each of them to notice two specific things: when they felt that child care and housecleaning were empty burdens and when they seemed like holy and humble acts of service to a higher purpose—a chance to take good care of precious and holy parts of creation.

A week later, Georgina said she'd had a strong reaction to the homework assignment. "I had always viewed housecleaning as a waste of time and diaper changing as an unpleasant chore. But when I began to look at each section of the house as a chance for me to create a more livable and sacred space for all three of us to live and grow, it made me want to do a little more to clean up the messiness. And when I began to see each moment of bathing Jenna, reading to Jenna, or picking up after Jenna as an act of holy service, it brought tears to my eyes. I might never be as skillful as Alice at noticing dust or making everything orderly, but I feel so much more involved now in making this a special and healthy living environment for the three of us."

To which Alice smiled and said, "I also noticed something shift this week as a result of looking at household issues from a spiritual viewpoint. I was wondering why Georgina had been helping so much more this past week. I noticed several times that she was doing a great job at things I've always done on my own. It's the first time since we moved in together that I've felt we were truly on the same team, and it's made me a lot less uptight about my whole orderliness obsession."

Alice admitted, "I guess for me there was always a lot of pride and ego in wanting my home to look impressive for guests, almost like a personal advertisement for who I am and what I can do in interior design. But this week I started to shift from that ego or pride viewpoint, and I began to feel a strong sense of gratitude for what Georgina and I have built together. We have a solid relationship, we have the joy of raising a fascinating kid, and we have an imperfect, slightly messy, but quite attractive living space. That's a lot to be thankful for."

HOUSEHOLD TEAMWORK AS AN ACT OF KINDNESS

There is one more way to make sure your differing styles and attitudes about household chores don't weaken your relationship but actually improve your closeness and mutual respect. It involves surprising your partner with kindness and consideration.

Sometimes the nicest gift you can give anxious or stressed-out partners is to let them call the shots in an area they care about strongly. The following stories demonstrate ways of dealing with household chores that show that partners care about each other.

Karl knows his wife, Yelena, gets tense when guests come for a dinner party or a family holiday gathering. So even though Karl doesn't give a hoot about dust or tidiness, he's willing to help out and put in a few hours of housecleaning and running errands to help Yelena whenever they're having guests.

According to Karl, "For me it's just a way of telling my wife I love her. Even though I was raised by my father and three older brothers to never let a woman boss me around, I don't see it as Yelena bossing me around. When I help her get the house ready according to her demanding specifications, it feels like we're a team. Even if she micro-manages, who cares? Our dinner parties and family gatherings have a lot of warmth and are good times."

According to Yelena, "It's such a gift that Karl helps without my having to beg or whine. At those moments when I see him making things easier for me to create some kind of order and beauty in the house, I feel like I'm with the best partner in the world."

Sara knows that her boyfriend Daniel is obsessive about keeping the inside of his car spotless. Yet Sara admits, "I have no interest in keeping my own car neat. In fact, for me a car is like a purse on wheels with all my stuff packed in haphazardly. But, with Daniel's car, I'm willing to improvise a little and become more of a neat freak, because it's my way of saying to him, 'I do care about you and I'm willing to put in a little extra effort to do what matters to you, even if it's not something that matters very much to me.'"

Ralph is very concerned about interior design and would enjoy an uncluttered, minimalist style in his home. Yet for almost five years he's been in a relationship with Mitch, who tends to be oblivious and unconcerned about how their home looks. In counseling, Ralph admitted, "There are times when I've tried to preach to Mitch that he's got to become more considerate and more conscious about the way our place looks. But it's like trying to teach a tone-deaf person how to sing."

I mentioned this fourth alternative to Ralph and Mitch by suggesting, "What if you surprised each other every so often by doing what the other person would want?"

For Mitch that meant picking up his socks, T-shirts, and underwear from the pile next to the bed and tossing them into the laundry hamper, or washing the dishes soon after eating a meal (rather than hours later or the next day) on the nights Ralph did the cooking.

For Ralph, giving a "gift" to Mitch consisted of allowing Mitch's housecleaning habits to be "good enough" every so often.

For example, after an especially stressful day Mitch wanted to let the dishes soak in the sink for a few hours before he washed them; Ralph decided to just relax and not make any critical or sarcastic remarks. When Mitch left the toothpaste tube open in the bathroom, Ralph took a deep breath and told himself, "No big deal," especially since Mitch had been picking up the clothes next to the bed more frequently.

Like many couples I have counseled, Ralph and Mitch learned to stop arguing over whose style of household management is "right" and to begin surprising one another with mutual acceptance and less criticism, sarcasm, and judgment. Instead of snapping at each other, they decided to become teammates with a sense of generosity and acceptance about their respective ways of being.

As Ralph explained during their final counseling session, "Our relationship got much better when I stopped preaching to Mitch that he should become as focused as I am on reducing clutter. Now we're more likely to laugh and appreciate how different we are. A few days ago I came home and Mitch announced, 'Hey, guess what! Our house is spotless and you didn't even have to ask.' That felt great. I don't need him to be that way all the time. Yesterday I came home and the house was a mess because Mitch is working on a huge assignment for an important client. I took a breath and said to Mitch, 'Hey, guess what! The house is a mess and I'm not even upset.'"

Ralph recalls, "At that moment, Mitch looked at me like I was ill or something and he asked, 'Are you sure you can be okay with this kind of clutter for a couple more days?' I laughed and said,

'Don't worry. If I start to get a rash or a cold sweat, I'll call the paramedics.'"

Mitch adds, "For the first time in years, we can just laugh and enjoy the fact that we have opposing styles. Yet we know we're both making progress to respect each other's right to be different. If we keep that in mind, our relationship is going to stay strong for a very long time."

RESOLVING FRUSTRATIONS
BEFORE THEY GET UGLY

How long has it been since you and your partner had a highly charged disagreement? A week? A day? Five minutes? Clashes are bound to happen in any relationship. But a strong disagreement between you and your partner may either be the beginning of serious trouble or the start of a wonderful breakthrough that takes your relationship to a deeper level of understanding.

Since this is a book about improving relationships, we need to talk about how to constructively handle being upset. Even in a sensible and well-matched couple, there will be moments when partners get irritated or angry with each other, particularly leading up to the moment of clarity when one or both wake up to the realization that their arguing MO doesn't always work because it sometimes leaves an unpleasant aftertaste for one or both of you.

In your own relationship, what happens when you or your partner get deeply hurt? Do you sometimes raise your voice and say harsh things you later regret? Does one of you give or get the silent treatment? Do you slam doors, break things, or threaten each other with the intensity of your anger?

I want to assure you that it's quite normal for two loving people to get on each other's nerves every so often. It's okay to have strong disagreements and differing ways of doing things. But if your clashes are frequent or include many hurtful responses that leave a lingering aftertaste, something has to change or the relationship will begin to crumble. It's crucial to find better ways to resolve these frustrations and painful moments—before it's too late and one of you shuts down emotionally.

STYLES OF ANGER MANAGEMENT

Just as each human being has unique fingerprints, each of us also has unique and personal ways of dealing with anger. Some people keep it inside. Some people let it out in a controlled way. Some make an effort to keep their anger inside but it oozes out all over the place.

Unfortunately, most of the ways we have developed for expressing or suppressing our anger toward a loved one actually make the situation worse. See if any of the following styles sound like you or someone you know.

THE SMILING PRETENDER

Most people in our society learn to keep their anger and their hurt feelings well-hidden. So instead of appropriately letting your loved one know when you're upset or irritated about something important, you might smile uncomfortably or pretend to be fine when you're actually quite peeved. Or if a loved one does something that really gets on your nerves and then asks, "Are you upset with me?" you might deny it and say, "No, I'm not upset. Do I look upset?"

To get an idea of what I mean by a Smiling Pretender, try to recall the character played by Renée Zellweger in the film *Jerry Maguire*. Nearly every time her career-obsessed and self-absorbed boyfriend (played by Tom Cruise) did something hurtful or insensitive, Zellweger's character would smile an awkward, uncomfortable smile that made her look like she was on the verge of tears.

As a result, Jerry Maguire continued to be self-centered and oblivious to how much he was hurting his loved one. During the final dramatic scene, in which he insists he wants to be with her because she "completes" him, he still seems self-absorbed and inattentive to her needs.

To smile when you are hurting inside is a hard habit to break. Yet I've seen many women and men make significant progress once they started telling themselves the truth about when they were angry or upset. The next time you find yourself smiling awkwardly or saying, "Don't worry about me, I'm fine," admit to yourself, "Oh, yes, I am definitely capable of being a Smiling Pretender who keeps my needs a secret, even from the person who's trying to love me." Just that moment of honesty and insight will begin to help you break the habit.

THE DUMPER

At the opposite extreme is the person who unloads a pile of complaints whenever he or she gets frustrated. When you disappoint this individual, even by accident, you get dumped on with an accumulation of all the times when you've been less than perfect.

For instance, one of the couples I counsel are Diane, a film executive, and Bertina, a paralegal, who both have excellent memories for details. When either of them gets upset with the other, a long list of frustrations and past imperfections comes pouring out. Their arguments begin about one simple thing and then quickly escalate into several complicated issues.

Diane described it to Bertina this way: "It's hard for the two of us to resolve anything because, as soon as we get pissed off at each other, we bring in all sorts of additional gripes that make us both feel defensive and more upset than when we first sat down. We've got to cut this out or we'll just keep drifting farther apart."

The next time you are in an argument with your loved one and you start piling on some ugly and unrelated examples from the past, be aware that you are "dumping," which is a sure way of prolonging the argument and upping the nastiness. As I often say to my counseling clients, "When a fight begins, you have two choices. You can stick to the specific issue that needs to get resolved, or you can dump an assortment of old resentments. The fight will last ten or twenty times longer with each additional dump."

THE HIGHLY INTELLIGENT
BUT ONE-SIDED BLAMER

A third anger style that creates problems occurs when our brains tell us we're innocent and the other person is completely at fault. Have you ever felt 100 percent convinced during an argument that you were right and your partner was wrong, though you later found out that the issue was more complicated and that each of you had contributed to the problem? Have you ever blamed your partner for something and then later found that he or she was innocent or had very good intentions that you didn't understand at first?

This rush to judgment happens to all of us at one time or another, especially if we are highly intelligent. It occurs because the human brain is adept at building a case and quickly convincing us that we are right, even if the situation is complicated and an alternative viewpoint might also be valid. Even the most rational and intelligent person may be blind to his or her part in creating a problem; it's much easier to see how the other person caused the problem. It is easy to imagine yourself flawless or innocent, but this attitude is a blind spot that smart people must overcome if they want to improve their relationships.

The next time you and your loved one have a disagreement and you grab onto the idea that you're 100 percent right and your partner is 100 percent wrong, take a moment to admit, "My brain is playing tricks on me again. My brain is trying to tell me that I'm flawless and my partner is an idiot. Well, I did *not* fall in love with an idiot. I better listen carefully to my partner's point of view before I start acting all self-righteous and obnoxious again."

THE "YOU HURT ME SO NOW I'LL HURT YOU" TYPE

This fourth anger style is definitely the most popular choice for most couples. Here's what happens:

a. Most people will try to be civil when an argument or disagreement begins,

b. but if they sense the other person is on the attack or is being overly defensive, they snap back with verbal guns blazing, and

c. once the two people are going at it, they really know what to say to hurt one another.

Some couples escalate quickly from "I'm going to be civil and decent here" to "You hurt me so now I'll hurt you back." Other couples take longer before tossing aside civility and compassion and attacking with harsh words. In either case, the vengeful counterattack acts like kerosene and prolongs the fiery clash.

The next time you or your partner stop using a calm, gentle tone of voice, take a moment to admit, "We've got this habit of hurting each other. It's a dangerous habit that can tear down the good relationship we've been building." It's a habit that can be broken if you decide that your relationship, your kids, and your future deserve something better.

BETTER OPTIONS THAN OUT-OF-CONTROL ANGER

Now that we've looked at anger styles that make things worse, let's look at effective ways to deal with the frustrations and fiery moments that happen in even good relationships. I've found one particular method that works more than 80 percent of the time. I call it the Two-Sided Defuser, and it works because it's easy to implement and fair to both partners.

Here's how to use it successfully with your partner the next time you're in an argument or a disagreement that's on the verge of getting ugly:

CALL A TIME-OUT

As soon as one of you raises your voice, clenches your teeth, or begins to blame or be defensive, someone needs to call a time-out. Just as in a basketball or football game, when the team leaders huddle and talk before taking action, you point the fingers of one hand vertically upward into the horizontal flat palm of the other hand to form a T. You should also say the word "time-out" in a calm and nonthreatening voice. This isn't to cut off conversation but to get you and your partner talking like teammates and problem-solving allies instead of adversaries and competitors. The time-out should not be seen as an escape or an avoidance of the problem. Nor are you minimizing the genuine hurt feelings that both of you are experiencing. Rather, the brief time-out is a clear and effective way to improve the tone and cooperation of your conversation.

REMIND EACH OTHER THAT YOU HAVE LEGITIMATE POINTS OF VIEW

As soon as someone calls a time-out, there must be an immediate statement that this isn't about winning or outsmarting each other. This brief intermission is about finding a problem-solving method and a tone of discussion that is respectful to both sides.

Without criticizing or accusing your partner of anything, simply say the following magic words, which work even when both partners are hotter than El Paso in July: "We're both legitimately upset and we both have to cool down so we can find out what we each need in order to feel like partners again."

These magic words prevent ugly scenes because they accomplish three things simultaneously and immediately:

* Because there's no blame or one-upmanship in these words, they begin to defuse the vicious or self-righteous tone being used only a few seconds earlier. When you calmly say, "We're both legitimately upset," it stops the vicious cycle of attacks and counterattacks.

* The words "so we can find out what we each need in order to feel like partners again" establish immediately that the goal is to explore and respect both points of view and that neither side is allowed to dominate. It also reassures both of you that neither of you will be ignored.

* The words "we both have to cool down" remind each partner to lighten up a bit while avoiding accusing either partner of being the primary cause of the problem. On the other hand, if you were to say, "Don't be so angry," "Don't raise your voice to me," "How dare you talk like that," or "You're being controlling," these accusatory phrases tend to spray lighter fluid on the fire and cause additional rounds of self-righteousness and defensiveness.

But when you say, "We're both legitimately upset and we both have to cool down so we can find out what we each need in order to feel like partners again," there are no good guys or bad guys. There are just two vulnerable and basically decent partners who each deserve to be heard and respected.

"We're Both Pretty Intense When We Get Provoked"

To see how the Two-Sided Defuser method works, consider what happened to Olivia and Jonathan. They're both highly educated with strong opinions about certain issues. So when they disagree, the situation heats up quickly.

According to Olivia, "Jonathan is a nice guy most of the time, but he's relentless when he gets upset. He'll back you into a corner and keep repeating himself—demanding that you give in or apologize. To tell you the truth, I *would* apologize sometimes if he didn't act so obnoxious and patronizing."

Jonathan sees their arguments in a different light. He says, "I fell in love with Olivia because she's passionate, whereas my ex-spouse was essentially cold and not very sensual. But the downside of having a passionate partner is that when Olivia gets worked up about a disagreement we're having, she's often defensive and stubborn. She won't apologize or acknowledge the truth about what I'm saying, even if it's obvious that I'm right."

Olivia and Jonathan came into couples counseling because their seven-year-old daughter, Alyse, had been crying uncontrollably one night after overhearing an intense argument between her parents. As Olivia describes it, "Alyse was terrified that her parents might get divorced like many of her friends' parents have in the past few years. When we tried to reassure her that our marriage is strong, Alyse said, 'You're lying, Mom. If your marriage was strong, you and Daddy wouldn't have such ugly fights.'"

Jonathan admitted, "That was the moment we both realized we needed to do better at this. It's one thing to have nasty fights when it's just the two of us. I've always known we're both pretty intense when we're provoked by each other's defensiveness. But now we've got kids who can't possibly feel secure and healthy if they repeatedly hear their parents raising their voices so intensely. We've got to do something before there's permanent damage to the relationship or to the kids' sense of well-being."

When I explained the Two-Sided Defuser method to Olivia and Jonathan, they were skeptical at first. Jonathan asked, "Do you really think that calling a time-out and using certain phrases will cool down two intense people?"

I suggested they try it the next time they were feeling on the verge of a fight. The fight came just three days later when Olivia was feeding their infant son Matthew and she called out to Jonathan not to comb Alyse's hair so roughly. Jonathan quickly shouted back, "Don't tell me what to do!"

According to Jonathan, "I was pissed because we have a long-standing policy not to criticize each other in front of the kids. If I happen to be on duty and I'm combing Alyse's hair, then Olivia needs to stop micro-managing everything and just let me do it in my own imperfect way. Olivia should have apologized for butting in and then the fight would have been over in a few seconds."

Olivia explained, "I was upset because all I said was to be gentle with Alyse so you don't cause split ends and he went ballistic on me. There's no way I'm going to apologize when I was just offering a sensible piece of advice and Jonathan was being an ass in lashing back the way he did."

Normally, Olivia and Jonathan would have escalated the fight and spent hours or possibly days mad at each other. But instead they tried the Two-Sided Defuser method to see if it might help.

Within the first few seconds after their tempers had started to flare, Olivia looked at Jonathan and made a T with her right hand pointed upward and her left palm facing downward. Olivia said in her calmest voice, "Time-out. We're both legitimately upset and we both have to cool down so we can find out what we each need in order to feel like partners again."

Jonathan recalled, "At that moment I was tempted to say 'Screw you' and go right back to arguing. But there was something so decent and fair about Olivia calling 'time-out' and saying we both needed to cool down because we both might have a legitimate point of view. It no longer felt like the usual power struggle or me-versus-her debate about who's innocent and who's guilty. Instead, for that split second I saw that we truly are partners in raising our kids and trying to create a sane household. So I took a breath and said, 'That's fair. We'll take a quick time-out and we'll both cool down a bit.'"

TAKE TURNS FINDING OUT WHAT WILL MAKE IT BETTER NEXT TIME

Now we come to the best part of the Two-Sided Defuser process—the moment when the two of you turn the disagreement from something that pulls you apart into a reason to come together in a deeper and more successful partnership. This breakthrough will happen in 80 percent of your disagreements if you follow the time-out with five or ten minutes of brainstorming about what will work better next time.

There are a few important ground rules that must be followed:

* Don't attack your partner or build a case about how innocent you are and how guilty the other person is.
* Don't rehash old resentments. Save your old stories for the highly acclaimed memoirs you might write when you are well up in years.
* Brainstorm together and offer a few creative ideas on specific phrases or actions that might work better next time.
* Make sure both of you get a few minutes to offer suggestions of what *you* (not the other person) are willing to do differently next time to improve the situation. As they say in twelve-step programs, don't take someone else's inventory. Just offer up your own amends and your specific plan for improving your own imperfections.

In Olivia and Jonathan's case, the creative brainstorming started with Olivia suggesting, "I think what might work better next time is if I don't shout out to you but rather if I ask you to come over for a moment and I say gently to you, 'I'm concerned about split ends. I have a certain way of combing Alyse's hair and it's hard to watch someone else combing it in a different way.' Would that work better?"

Jonathan thought for a moment and replied, "If you say it like we're partners it'll probably work fine. Maybe it's because I grew up with two critical parents, but I do get defensive when someone tries to tell me what to do."

Then Jonathan offered his half of the brainstorming when he added, "As for me, I think what might work better next time is if I say to myself, 'Don't lose it in front of Alyse. Talk to Olivia later, when we're alone, and tell her she's got to allow me to brush Alyse's hair in my own imperfect way.' Would that work for you?"

Olivia thought for a moment and then said, "I like the part where you talk yourself into staying calm and you wait until we can talk about it patiently when we're alone. But I'm not sure I can keep my mouth shut if I see you unintentionally hurting Alyse because, in fact, her hair is very hard to comb and you might be accidentally giving her split ends. I know that might sound like I'm micro-managing again, but hey, I'm a mama bear and I have trouble staying silent if my baby girl is hurting."

Jonathan looked at his wife for a moment and said lovingly, "I know you're a mama bear and I'm glad you are. So let's make a new rule. If I'm causing split ends or hurting Alyse, you get to speak up. But you've got to talk to me like I'm your partner, not your enemy. On the other hand, if I'm being careful and I'm not giving her split ends, or if she's actually enjoying having me comb her hair gently, please let us have that time together."

Olivia smiled and said, "That's a good plan for next time."

Then they gave each other a knowing look and Olivia said, "I do love you, even if you're a pain sometimes." Jonathan kissed her and replied, "I love you, too, even if you do get a little intense sometimes."

As you can see from this example, the Two-Sided Defuser system doesn't ask you to check your brains or your sense of humor at the door. It simply cuts out the time-wasting, defensive speeches about how "I'm innocent, and you're completely at fault" that cause arguments to escalate out of control. This simple but powerful method keeps your arguments from getting ugly because it reminds you to call a time out, cool down, admit that you both have legitimate points of view, and then brainstorm as partners about what will make it better next time.

WHAT IF ONE OF YOU IS STILL UPSET?

For many couples, the peaceful back and forth brainstorming that Olivia and Jonathan did is not so easy. In many partnerships, one or both partners have a lot of fire inside, or a history of being pushed around, or a reluctance to cool down and trust that a fair solution will be reached.

Quite often I say to people who have strong tempers, "There's nothing wrong with being passionate, but it requires extra wisdom to handle the passion well. Without any judgment or guilt, let's just find out how long it usually takes for your brain and your blood pressure to cool down. When you're upset with your loved one, how much time (on average) do you require to relax and feel like partners again?"

I've found that each human being is different in how much time it takes to cool down. Some people need a half hour before their defensive, case-building thoughts calm down and they're ready to discuss a volatile issue calmly. Others need two hours before they can think clearly. Still others need to sleep on it overnight before they feel open and creative again.

Based on your best sense of your own temper and your partner's temper, how long would you say it usually takes before the angry feelings lighten up and you're ready to be partners again? There are no right or wrong, good or bad answers to this question. In fact, the sooner you and your partner stop judging your anger cycles and start telling the truth about how long a time out you need, the better your problem-solving teamwork will be.

"I Need to Be Alone So I Don't Say or Do Something I'll Regret"

Joanna and Luke are a good example of what can happen when you admit how long it takes your anger to subside. They've been together for three years and even though they're not married, they're truly partners. In fact, Luke has become an active and involved father for Joanna's two teenage sons, one of whom has Attention Deficit Hyperactivity Disorder.

Luke described their situation this way: "Things are never boring at our house. Joanna runs her mail-order business out of the

145

back bedroom. Her two sons are always getting into trouble. I have an extremely high-pressure job in the music business. And our relationship has always been like a roller coaster. One day Joanna and I are getting along wonderfully, and the next day we'll have an argument that quickly explodes into several hours of verbal sparring and nasty comments."

In couples counseling we discovered that the Two-Sided Defuser method might not be enough to calm down Joanna and Luke when their feelings get hurt in an argument. Joanna explained, "I've found that when Luke gets hurt or angry, there's no reasoning with him for a few hours. He slams doors, he throws things, and he even punched his fist into a mirror one night. I've also got quite a mouth when I'm upset, which only adds to the explosiveness.

"We love each other a lot and I know Luke has enough self-control so that he'll never hit me or the kids. But I'm concerned at how long our fights last and what a horrible example we're setting for my sons."

So I asked Joanna and Luke the question that was stated earlier, "Without any judgment or guilt, how long do you usually need before your blood pressure and your racing thoughts cool down? Based on your best sense of your own temper, how long does it usually take before the angry feelings lighten up and you're ready to be partners again?"

Joanna answered first. "I usually need just a few minutes, because once I've vented my feelings and said a few nasty things, I'm usually ready to cool down."

Luke thought for a moment and then answered, "I think I need a half hour and sometimes an entire hour if I'm really ticked off. At times like that, I just need to be alone so I don't say or do something I'll later regret. But the trouble is Joanna won't let me take a walk or cool down. As soon as I say, 'I need to get out of here,' she freaks out and accuses me of being irresponsible or of walking out on her."

For many couples, when one partner needs a ten-minute time-out, or a sixty-minute time-out, or a two-hour time-out to cool down, the other partner often feels afraid or upset that the angry partner is walking out. Yet I've found that the problem may be solved if the slower-to-cool-down partner reassures his or her loved one by saying, "I need an hour (or thirty minutes) and then I'll definitely be back in a much better frame of mind to work this out with you peacefully."

I asked Luke, "When you're upset, would you be able to reassure Joanna that you are definitely coming back in an hour in a much better frame of mind to work this out with her peacefully? Or is your anger at that moment so intense that you can't stop for a second to reassure her?"

Luke said, "I think that even when I'm extremely upset, I've still got some control. I know I have enough control not to physically hit her or the kids. So I probably have enough control to say a few reassuring words and remind her that I'm not bolting—I'm just taking a time-out so I can cool down and become reasonable again."

I asked Joanna, "Can you let him take a quiet time-out if he promises he'll be back with a much calmer way of talking?"

Joanna thought for a moment and said, "I wish he didn't need the time-out whatsoever because it's hard to wait for thirty minutes or an hour before we get to talk it over. But if that will help us cool things down, I guess I can let him go take a walk. If he'll be a lot more pleasant to deal with, let him get some fresh air and take that furious look off his face."

The very next week they tested it. Joanna was having a hard day with her sons. She called Luke at work to find out what time he would be home. He said he'd be home by six o'clock. When he wasn't home by seven, she was worried and upset. When he walked in at eight, she was furious.

As Luke recalled it, "I had busted my chops to cut short two important meetings so I could get home and help with the kids. Then I hit some ridiculous traffic, and I tried to call on the cell phone to let Joanna know I'd be late. But the line was continually busy so all I could do was leave messages that I guess she never heard. Anyway, the minute I walked in the door, instead of a warm hello, she was livid and she didn't hold back at all. She told me I don't love her, I don't care about her kids, I can't be trusted, blah blah blah!"

Within a few minutes of walking in the door, Luke was losing his temper. He remembers, "I wanted to shut her up somehow or throw something. But I also knew this was my first chance to try out the thing we'd discussed last week. So I said to Joanna, 'Sweetheart, I need just a half hour to cool down and then I'll definitely be able to work this out with you from a much better frame of mind. Thirty minutes. No more. No less. Can you give me that so I won't have to be all cranky and short-tempered with you?'"

Joanna described her reaction. "There was a part of me that wanted to say, 'Forget your thirty minutes. You're already two hours late and now you want another thirty minutes to cool yourself down?' But I looked at him and realized he absolutely was telling me the truth. He really needed his thirty friggin' minutes. If I could chill for just thirty minutes, he would be a helluva lot easier to talk with and I would finally get the relief I needed."

Joanna continued, "So I let him take a brisk walk around the neighborhood, and this time I didn't hound him or call him names. I just said sweetly, 'See you in thirty,' and it worked. Exactly thirty minutes later he walked in much more relaxed and reasonable. Then we did the Two-Sided Defuser steps we discussed a few weeks ago, and it took us only a few minutes to realize that we both were a little overcooked from very stressful days and we both wanted to be partners in raising these two sons and giving each other relief. It was the shortest fight we'd ever had, and I hope Luke doesn't mind my saying that we had great sex later that night as well."

COOLING DOWN AT THE MOST FRUSTRATING MOMENTS

If you or your partner has a temper that requires ten minutes, thirty minutes, sixty minutes, two hours, or an entire night in separate rooms to calm, don't put each other down for it. Your fire is probably a good thing in certain areas of your life—possibly it fuels your creativity, your passion for living, your sensuality, or your intense loyalty to people or issues. But your fire also needs to be managed properly, and it may require a substantial prearranged time-out for you to cool it down.

Here are a few guidelines to keep in mind during the time-out moments:

When you are apart from each other during a mutually agreed-upon time-out, don't let your brain build a case against your partner. Talk back to your brain and say, "This is not about proving who's right and who's wrong. This is about cooling down and becoming respectful partners again."

Make sure you get some oxygen during the time-out. For some people that means taking a brisk walk or a run. For others it means breathing in and out, slowly and calmly. For still others it means praying, meditating, doing yoga, or writing in a journal while breathing gently.

Remember that the goal of the time-out is to regain your clarity of mind so that you don't keep acting up on your loved one or escalating the ugliness between you. You can make a lot of progress if you just say to yourself, "There are no good guys or bad guys here—we're just two basically decent and vulnerable people who are both legitimately upset and we have to cool down so we can find out what we each need in order to feel like partners again."

If you have trouble recalling these Two-Sided Defuser words when you're upset, do what many of my counseling clients have done: Write them on a small note card and put the note card in your wallet where you can find it quickly during a heated moment.

Then read the card slowly to yourself as you take deep breaths. Even a fiery and intense person can usually cool down if the note card is read slowly two or three times during the time-out.

When the time-out is over, remember that you are about to speak to your beloved partner. This person's soul and your soul are connected in deep and mysterious ways. You are journeying through life with this individual. Don't try to prove how innocent you are and how guilty the other person is. Just accept that you each are vulnerable and you both need calm voices and an open heart in order to work together peacefully. Good luck!

STEP SIX

DEALING WITH CHALLENGING PEOPLE WHO ARE PART OF THE PACKAGE

I'll bet you didn't anticipate when you first became attracted to your current partner that he or she might bring some challenging characters into your life. Maybe there's a mother-in-law or father-in-law who tests your patience. Or an ex-spouse or ex-lover who tends to stir up trouble. Or kids from a previous relationship who haven't fully accepted you yet. Or a troubled sibling or friend who keeps asking for money, and you're never sure where to set the limit. Or some family member or old friend you can't stand, but your partner feels obligated to see him or her often. Or a flirtatious co-worker or friend who simply won't recognize the TAKEN sign on your partner's heart.

When you fall in love with someone and want to spend your life with the person, one of the mysteries is how the two of you will deal with meddlesome or troublesome people who come with the package. In almost every relationship there are family members on both sides who may make things stressful at times.

As you think about the challenging people and situations that

153

you and your partner have brought to the mix, do you recall some difficult moments in recent months or years?

* Is there someone in your partner's family, circle of friends, or work life who seems to have so much clout with and influence over your partner that you wonder if your partner will ever stand up for you and your relationship?

* Is there a troubled or hard-to-deal-with person on your side or your partner's side who needs a lot of attention and understanding?

* Is there someone in your partner's life who seems determined to paint you in a bad light?

* Are there times when your partner says yes to a family obligation or social invitation and you aren't given a chance to say what *you* might prefer?

* Is there someone that your partner flirts with or has sexual chemistry with, and is it beginning to get on your nerves?

* Are there times when your way of doing things and your in-laws' ways are in opposition, and you feel caught in the middle?

* Is there an old friend, a co-worker, an ex-spouse, an ex-lover, or a family member who has never quite accepted that you and your partner are meant to be together, or who treats one of you with disrespect?

* Is there a child, teenager, or young adult from your current or previous relationship who is masterful at getting one of

you to say yes to something for which the other partner has already said no?

* Is there someone in your family or in your partner's family who wants to change your religious beliefs, political preferences, or basic core self, and do you sometimes wonder if your partner sides with this person and not with you?

* Are there recurring arguments or debates between you and your partner because you disagree about whether to speak up or remain silent around certain relatives, friends, and co-workers who say or do offensive things?

A PROBLEM THAT CANNOT BE IGNORED

If someone in your respective families or circle of friends is causing arguments or hurt feelings, don't minimize or downplay the importance of resolving these issues. I have seen hundreds of couples whose relationships were harmed or destroyed because they were unwilling or unable to come up with creative solutions for handling divisive individuals. It's essential that you and your partner have a heart-to-heart conversation about how you will sustain your bond when someone is knowingly or unknowingly doing things to split you apart.

There are three ways to make sure that your closeness and trust don't get damaged by others: plan ahead of time with your partner how you will deal with problems and stay united; listen to your partner's concerns; and end any flirtations you are nurturing—now!

PLAN AHEAD FOR DEALING WITH PROBLEMS

Most couples wait until they're in the middle of a huge fight or a shouting match before they discuss how to deal with a situation that has been testing their unity and sanity. They wait until the angriest and least productive moment to talk about something that is better explored when they are calmer and more reasonable.

When you know you will be seeing a difficult family member at Thanksgiving, Christmas, Hanukkah, Kwanzaa, Easter, Passover, a birthday party, a wedding, or some other event, you have two choices:

a. wait until you've been slimed by this divisive individual and you're so furious that you snap at your partner and say, "I hate your crazy family," or

b. plan ahead with your partner to figure out how you are going to deal with this person differently so you can support each other and stay unified no matter what the difficult family member does.

Even though most couples choose the first option, I strongly recommend you consider the second option. That means sitting down with your beloved partner or taking a relaxing walk in nature and saying, "Let's talk about how we can stay strong and unified even when your _____ tries to drive a wedge between us at the next family event."

The purpose of this proactive conversation is not to attack your mate and his or her dysfunctional family. During workshops and radio interviews for my earlier book, *When Difficult Relatives Happen to Good People*, I often advised people not to get into arguments about whose family is crazier. It's a conversation that goes nowhere. In addition, don't assume that because your partner says harsh things about his or her family that this entitles you to say the same exact things about them. If your partner says, "I hate my self-absorbed father. He's a complete jerk," that does *not* mean you can call your partner's father a self-absorbed jerk. It means shut up and listen without putting your foot in your mouth, because in most cases your partner will get defensive if you bad-mouth his or her flesh and blood.

For some reason, we feel a sense of relief when we criticize our own relatives, but we often feel offended when a spouse or lover makes the same comments. Couples need to be careful not to criticize each other's less-than-perfect loved ones (even if the criticism is 100 percent accurate) because the goal in a relationship is to support one another in improving things, not to dissect or analyze how messed up your loved one's family might be. So instead of blasting your partner's family or calling them names, work together on ways to stay unified through the ups and downs of your close encounters of the family kind.

"I Thought by Now Your Kids and Your Mom Would Be More Accepting"

Arnie and Maureen are a perfect example of how important it is to have a productive planning talk before you're in a tiff and to choose carefully what you say about your partner's less-than-perfect loved ones. Arnie was only thirty-nine years old with three young children when his wife Josie died of ovarian cancer. Three years later he met Maureen at a volunteer event and they began dating.

As Arnie recalled, "I was very nervous at first to introduce Maureen to my children because they were not quite ready for someone other than their mother to be with me. I also was concerned that my own aging mother, who's an extremely opinionated and demanding person, might be hesitant to welcome someone else into our family, especially because she liked Josie a lot. Yet I knew that I'd found in Maureen a wonderful partner, and after several years of being alone I had to get on with my life."

According to Maureen, "I knew within a few weeks after we'd met that falling in love with Arnie was going to have some complications because of his three children and his mom; they were very cold and rude to me the first few times we got together. At first I said playfully, 'How come your mom is such a bitch?' but I could see from the hurt look on Arnie's face that, even though he would call his mother the *b*-word, he wasn't comfortable if I said the same thing."

Maureen continued, "Then I tried to bite my tongue for several months and I put up with a lot of disrespect and harsh comments from each of the kids and from Arnie's mother. I told Arnie we needed to see a counselor, but he refused. I told him that I needed him to be stronger in letting his kids and his mother know that I'm a human being and that even if they don't love me they can still be decent and civil."

But Arnie just kept saying, "Don't worry, it'll get better with time." Yet after more than a year of dating Arnie and putting up with some very unpleasant family gatherings, Maureen couldn't keep silent any longer. One night her feelings just poured out as she said, "I don't think I can take this anymore! I thought by now your kids and your mom would be more accepting. But they're not making any progress, and you're not doing very much to stand up for someone you claim to love."

That started a painful argument where Arnie got defensive and said, "I can't believe you don't understand how hard this is for all of us" and Maureen replied, "I do understand that each of you worships Josie like she's some kind of saint. But let me tell you, I'm sure she wasn't perfect all the time, and this family has got to wake up at some point and realize that life goes on."

To which Arnie remarked, "Well, your family is just as screwed up, so I don't think you've got a right to start telling me what's wrong with my family."

Maureen responded sarcastically, "Well, excuse me! I was just repeating what I've heard you say. You've admitted to me that one of the problems is that everyone has put Josie on a pedestal because she's no longer alive. How come you can say that with no problem and yet when I repeat it back you look furious?"

Arnie was still fuming as he replied, "It's one thing if I feel like saying my kids and my mom need to stop living in the past. But I certainly don't want to hear that from you. And don't you dare start telling me how to feel about my wife. You've crossed a line you don't want to cross, do you understand?"

Maureen had tears streaming down her face as she said, "Oh, yes, I understand perfectly. . . ."

A few days later, Arnie and Maureen showed up in my office because they realized that holding it all inside or criticizing each other's families was getting them nowhere. So we began to work together on having a productive planning conversation.

Like most couples, Arnie and Maureen had made the mistake of waiting until they were both furious before they tried to talk about the most substantial obstacle in their otherwise good relationship. So I told them, "Even though you both have busy lives, you need to initiate these important conversations when you're in a good mood and you're open to exploring creative solutions."

I asked Arnie and Maureen to set aside an hour on their own that weekend to take a relaxing walk so they could explore calmly what kind of support and teamwork they could offer each other to get through this painful family dilemma. I told them, "It's common for people to start criticizing and bad-mouthing each other's imperfect loved ones when a situation is hard to resolve. But let's not do that this time. Let's make sure that when you take a walk this weekend you're brainstorming possible solutions together. That means you will not look at each other as the cause of the problem, but as your supportive teammate and best friend who wants to help deal with a painful issue that isn't either person's fault. Remember that neither of you caused Josie to die. Neither one of you is to blame for the fact that Arnie's kids and his mom were very attached to Josie and that they're having trouble imagining that life will continue in a new form. As with most family dilemmas, this isn't about blaming or criticizing—it's about coming up with creative ways to support each other and stay unified while dealing with situations that we can't fully control."

The next week, Maureen and Arnie told me what had happened during their relaxing walk on a beautiful, shady street. Maureen explained, "I was nervous that this subject was too volatile to talk about. But I found to my surprise that Arnie was much more helpful and supportive when I avoided saying anything critical about his loved ones. Instead, I just asked for his ideas on what might improve the situation and how we could stay close and supportive through the process of merging our two worlds."

Arnie added, "I think what made this conversation different is that we set up a tone of being on the same team and working together instead of against each other. Maureen asked me in a calm voice, 'What might help the kids feel safer to talk about their full range of feelings about our relationship? Of course they wish you were still with their mom. Of course they want to be loyal to their mom and not be too friendly to a newcomer. Of course they aren't comfortable seeing you as a vulnerable person with your own sexual and social needs beyond your role as their father. But let's be on the same team in all this. Let's find a loving way to help your kids realize that we understand these normal reactions and that they can have these reluctant feelings while still being decent and respectful to this newcomer their dad loves and wants to be with.'"

Arnie continued, "When Maureen spoke in such a caring and

nonjudgmental way about my kids' legitimate feelings, it made me love her even more. I realized that this is not an issue of Maureen versus me, or Maureen versus the kids, or Maureen versus my mom. This is about all of us together having to deal with some very confusing and deep feelings."

That relaxing walk and productive planning conversation were the beginning of a breakthrough in Maureen and Arnie's relationship. Over the next few weeks, Arnie had a couple of heart-to-heart talks with each of his kids and with his mother about how he appreciated their mixed emotions and didn't want to rush them or tell them what to feel. But he was strong and clear for the first time as he explained to his mother and his children that "even if you still have some concerns about Maureen, you still must be decent and respectful in this complicated situation. You don't need to be phony, but I expect you to treat this good person with caring and kindness. Are you willing to do that?"

After Arnie explained this to each of his loved ones and listened to their reactions, his mother and his children began to make some progress. Arnie concluded, "I think my mom and my kids were waiting for me to give them a clear indication that it's possible to be loyal to Josie's memory while being gracious and warm toward Maureen. They needed to hear that I will always honor Josie's importance in our lives and, at the same time, that we can welcome Maureen into our family. I calmly explained to them several times that I will continue to be close and very involved with each of them, even though I'm deeply in love with Maureen as well. I sensed I was making some progress when my eldest daughter said,

'Dad, I want you to be happy. And I believe Mom would also want you to be happy and not alone.'"

If your own relationship is complicated because two families are merging, or because family members are feeling that they have to remain loyal to the way things were, please make sure that the blaming, criticizing, and verbal attacks are stopped immediately. Set aside some relaxed time to plan with your partner what you can do as teammates to improve the situation. How will you make sure you stay caring and respectful of each other's families when other people are trying to pull you apart? In most cases, these planning conversations will not only address the current crisis but also strengthen your relationship because there's nothing quite as wonderful as knowing that you're committed to helping each other no matter what.

TAKE YOUR PARTNER'S CONCERNS SERIOUSLY

When your partner feels slighted or jealous of the attention you are giving someone in your family, at work, or in your circle of friends, your first response might be, "Oh, you shouldn't feel that way." But maybe there is some merit to his or her point of view. Maybe you do jump to attention nearly every time a certain relative, co-worker, or friend calls. Or maybe you have been far too willing to say to your partner, "I can't be there for you right now. There's a crisis [in your family, at work, or with a friend] that I have to deal with right now." Or maybe you don't realize how completely involved you get with certain high-drama or high-status people while taking your beloved partner for granted.

"I Feel like an Outsider and I Wish I Could Disappear"

Bonnie and Evelyn's case illustrates what works and what doesn't work when one partner is feeling slighted. They met in college and have been together for almost eight years in a mostly good relationship. Bonnie is a ceramic artist and preschool teacher. Evelyn is an attorney in her third year with a prestigious law firm.

According to Bonnie, "Every few weeks there is another obligatory law firm event that Evelyn needs me to attend with her. A fundraiser, a dinner party at a partner's home, or a night of wining and dining an important client or the interns and first-year associates. Evelyn literally shines at these events. She always looks great and she knows how to schmooze the partners so she can build alliances in the firm. She loves talking about the intricacies of cases and exchanging office gossip."

Bonnie continued, "As for me, I feel like an outsider and I wish I could disappear. I know Evelyn cares about me, but at these events she sometimes ignores me for the entire three hours we're there because she's so busy working the room and scoring points for her career. I try to find someone to talk to. But there is nothing quite like attempting to have a conversation with a law firm big shot who asks, 'So, what do you do?' I'll say I'm a ceramic artist and I teach preschool. Within a half second, the big shot has a 'get me away from this loser' look on his face and he's moving on to someone who can give him a *real* topic of conversation—like golf swings, stock tips, or 'how 'bout them Lakers?'"

Evelyn disagreed somewhat and commented, "Bonnie's being

dramatic again. First of all, I don't ignore her for three hours. I do check in every so often, but I'm not going to spend my whole time taking care of my partner. I expect that Bonnie is quite capable of taking care of herself and finding someone interesting to talk to at these events. Bottom line, these social occasions are very important if I'm going to be made partner in the next year or two. I've never said this before because I didn't want to hurt Bonnie's feelings, but if we want to be financially secure some day, Bonnie needs to get over it and stop being such a wuss."

Bonnie was upset as she replied, "Well, screw you, too, Ms. Social Butterfly. Not all of us are gifted with the talent of being world-class bullshitters!"

To which Evelyn replied, "Like I said, you need to get over it. I need you to take care of yourself when I'm at a work-related event."

Like many couples where one partner feels ignored and the other partner wishes he or she would "get over it," Bonnie and Evelyn were at risk of ruining an otherwise good relationship because of their differing ways of dealing with social situations. So I asked Evelyn, "What if you're both right to some extent on this issue? What if Bonnie is correct in saying it's painful to be the only artist/teacher in a room full of lawyers, and you're correct in saying that this is very important for your career and future financial security? Instead of blaming each other, what if you were allies in trying to find a solution that works for each of you?"

Evelyn replied quickly, "Like what? How exactly am I going to build work alliances and at the same time make sure Bonnie isn't feeling abandoned or slighted?"

I said, "That's the question we need to address. How exactly can you both get some of what you need at these social events? Let's come up with some creative and unusual solutions that might satisfy both of you."

As with most couples, when the focus becomes not who's to blame but what innovative solutions might work for both individuals, some good ideas emerged. First, Bonnie and Evelyn smiled at each other as if to call a truce in their verbal sparring. Evelyn said, "One of the reasons we've been together eight years is that we both know how to dish it out and take it when we're upset."

Then Bonnie and Evelyn suggested various creative ways that they could both get what they needed at work-related social events. Bonnie began the brainstorming process by saying, "Maybe we ought to think about these law firm events like a prom for grown-ups. There's some mingling, some gossiping, some strange rituals, and some catching up with your classmates, but you should dance at least a few times with the one who put the bouquet on your wrist. I don't need you to sit next to me or to spend the entire time with me. But if we could have a five- or ten-minute check-in once an hour, plus a fifteen-minute private conversation or a walk at some point during the event to catch up, that might be enough."

Evelyn added, "We could also have a few secret signals for checking in. For instance, if I look across the room at you and you're having a good conversation with someone interesting, you could simply scratch your right ear. But if you're stuck listening to a boring or arrogant law firm partner, or if you've completely run out of people to talk to, you could scratch your left eyebrow. The left eyebrow scratch means 'Get your butt over here right now. I've fallen and I can't get up!'"

Bonnie thought that would work fine, but asked about the ten- or fifteen-minute walk and private talk during the event. Evelyn paused for a moment and said with some humor in her voice, "I'll agree to it because I'm such a decent human being." Bonnie smiled and added, "And humble, too!"

As you can see, the more you take each other's concerns seriously (and stop saying, "You shouldn't feel that way!" or "Get over it!"), the quicker you can cook up a workable solution. Many couples struggle with this issue of one partner feeling slighted or left out at work-related events, family gatherings, or social events where one partner is welcomed and the other is treated like an outsider. Rather than calling your partner names or starting a fight, this would be a great opportunity to come up with creative and unusual ways to support each other at these difficult moments.

END A FLIRTATION NOW

Flirtation is the third issue that sometimes flares up with couples. In nearly every long-term relationship, there are likely to be at least a few moments when one or both partners feel attracted to someone else. It might be a co-worker, a stranger on an out-of-town trip, or someone in your circle of friends who flirts with one of you. Or maybe an old flame reappears in your life and your partner feels uncomfortable. Or perhaps one of you has some sexual chemistry with someone or a bit of a crush on someone and it's starting to become a problem in your relationship.

If a flirtation has started to distract you or your partner, don't panic! There are healthy ways to regain the unity and trust before it's too late. It doesn't mean the relationship is doomed. Rather, it usually means you are both sensual human beings who need to clarify the invisible line of safety that shouldn't be crossed.

Since nearly every relationship needs some clear agreement as to what's safe and what's not safe, I recommend that the best time to clarify the specific "flirtation ground rules" of your partnership is when the two of you are getting along or in a good mood. It shouldn't be a harsh or accusatory conversation, just a healthy clarification of what you are comfortable with (or not comfortable with) when it comes to flirtations and feeling attracted to other people.

That means taking a relaxing stroll together or sitting down with a counselor and honestly talking about this issue in a way that can strengthen your relationship now and in the future. Even if you think it could never happen to you or your partner, it's still a good idea to explore in your own hearts and discuss openly these questions:

* What's it like for you when a stranger or friend looks at you or your partner (or talks to one of you) in a way that indicates this person is interested in more than a nonsexual friendship? Based on your own particular concerns and feelings, at what point is this a harmless event and at what point is it dangerous or disrespectful of your relationship?

* Is there a type of flirtation or sensuality (dressing in an attractive way, dancing with someone else, having outside friendships, hugging or being affectionate with someone else) that your partner has done that you were comfortable with and that didn't make you feel jealous, insecure, left out, or taken for granted?

* Is there a type of flirtation or sensuality that your partner has done that you were nervous about or that made you feel a loss of trust toward your partner?

* Is there a serious flirtation or a crush developing with someone (either for you or for your partner) that needs to be discussed and dealt with before it causes problems in your relationship?

* Is there a confusion for either partner about what constitutes a safe and appropriate glance, conversation, or degree of involvement with an attractive stranger, friend, or co-worker, and what constitutes trouble or a breaking of trust?

* What should you do if an interesting stranger, friend, or co-worker is starting to occupy too much of your sensual or romantic thoughts?

* What should you do if you suspect that your partner is starting to look elsewhere?

I've found that the most successful long-term couples are those who clarify and deeply consider these vitally important trust and safety issues with each other. It's not a question of criticizing, possessing, or controlling one's partner, but rather of strengthening the bond and the warmth between the two of you.

"I Do Want to Trust You, But . . ."

Joel and Laureen are a good-looking couple I counseled at several points in their relationship because they needed help in clarifying their individual flirtation ground rules. The first time they called for counseling was a month before their wedding. Joel's college buddy and best man had arranged an extravagant Vegas-style bachelor party for Joel and his twelve closest male friends. Laureen was worried when she heard there might be half-naked female dancers. Joel kept insisting, "You shouldn't worry. It's no big deal. You're being ridiculous."

Joel's dismissive comments made Laureen even more concerned. As she explained, "It's one thing to know my husband-to-be will be drooling over some woman with porn-star dimensions. But now, in addition, I'm hearing him say 'You're being ridiculous,' which makes me wonder if Joel is as decent and caring a person as I'd hoped he would be."

I kept silent at first to see how Laureen and Joel were going to negotiate a solution to this common conflict. Laureen suggested to Joel, "I don't want to be the one to tell you and your friends not to have a good time. But I don't feel comfortable if the dancers let you touch them. The last thing I want is for your 'don't worry' bachelor party to leave us with sexually transmitted diseases or feelings of distrust that could last a lot longer than one night."

Joel replied, "Trust me on this. You don't have to worry. I

won't be touching anyone or exchanging any bodily fluids with a stranger. I'm not stupid."

Laureen said, "I do want to trust you. But I assume you'll be drinking and there will be a lot of pressure from your friends and from the women who are encouraged to push the limits and give the groom and best man their money's worth."

To which Joel asked, "Do you really think any of these women could possibly cause me to love you less or make me want to leave you?"

Laureen thought for a moment and said, "To be honest, no! I'm not worried that you're gonna leave me for one of the dancers at your bachelor party. But I'm worried that you're going to have this woman's incredible figure somewhere in your mind on our honeymoon. Or that you're going to have some of her saliva or worse traveling through your bloodstream and give me an infection as a wedding present. Most of all, I'm worried that there will be a few lies, a few cover-ups, and some unfinished business from this bachelor party that will linger in our heads. Or that this might be the first of many times when you'll tell me what you think I want to hear. That's no way to build the trust you and I will need to make this marriage last a lifetime."

At that moment, I interrupted and asked them to look at the flirtation ground rule questions listed above. I said, "Rather than arguing, take turns being honest with each other about what feels comfortable and what feels uncomfortable about this very complicated issue. That means you can co-design, as equal partners, the flirtation ground rules for your particular relationship."

As soon as we began looking at the questions, Joel offered that he's probably not completely consistent on this issue. He admitted, "Sometimes when Laureen looks hot and I see men staring at her, I feel proud. But at other times I do feel insecure that one of these days she might get interested in someone else or let some guy impress her with his money or his charm."

Laureen then commented, "For me, there's a slightly different concern. I usually don't worry when I hear Joel tell me that one of the secretaries at his office has been giving him lingering looks. I trust that Joel wouldn't jeopardize our marriage or his career by hitting on one of the secretaries. But I do worry when Joel has a few drinks in him, because I've seen him become impulsive and defiant when he's feeling no pain from two glasses of wine or beer."

Joel replied, "We do have to find a way to trust each other. I don't want some affair to split us apart."

As the conversation continued, Joel and Laureen began to see that this technique of carefully co-designing their flirtation ground rules was drawing them closer together. After a few minutes, Joel commented, "I have to admit it bugged me at first to hear Laureen trying to influence my bachelor party. But the truth is that both of us are extremely vulnerable on this issue. We're both decent looking and we're both going to have times when someone tests us to see if our marriage vows are real or a joke."

Then he looked at Laureen and said, "You know, this bachelor party decision is boiling down to a choice that I need to think about. The issue is not whether my wife-to-be is going to veto the plans that my best man has made. It's really about whether I should indulge one last fling with my buddies that might leave some long-lasting mistrust and pain between us. I definitely don't like being told what I can and cannot do, but I'm not going to lie and tell you that dancers and a lot of liquor won't turn into a problem. I do want to be a trustworthy partner and I can't promise I'll make the right decisions when I'm loaded and an experienced troublemaker is rubbing up next to me and trying to push me over the line. So I'm gonna have to think this over and see what else I can do with my buddies that won't cause any harm to our marriage."

Laureen looked at him and you could see the renewed respect she felt for Joel. She said nothing for a moment, but then she took his hand and said, "I don't want to control you or tell you what to do. And I'm glad you're gonna think this over and come up with something you feel solid about."

A few weeks later, Joel and his best man hosted an all-night bachelor party that included incredible food, a lot of laughs, some intense card games, and one outrageous treat that Joel described to Laureen as follows: "We rented a porn film that we showed in reverse motion with stop-action freeze frames. It had everybody in stitches. Most of us were laughing so hard our stomachs hurt. And I was dealt several good hands around 3:00 A.M. and ended up winning more than two hundred dollars. The party was a huge success."

Laureen was only slightly grossed out. Mostly she felt extremely good that Joel had taken her concerns seriously and that he'd designed a bachelor party that was fun but safe.

As she said later, during their first counseling session as a married couple, "This showed me that Joel has the courage to dig down deep and find out what's really important for our relationship. And that he's willing to stand up to his friends and say, 'I do care about my wife and our marriage,' even when his friends are pressuring him in a different direction."

"We've Got a New Problem on the Same Issue as Before"

I didn't hear from Joel and Laureen for almost five years after that session. But then one day they wanted to come in for additional counseling. As I learned from Joel, "We've got a new problem on the same issue as before. Only this time it's Laureen who's having trouble staying within the flirtation ground rules."

Laureen then described how she had become quite isolated and lonely after the birth of their first child, Emma. Laureen admitted, "I was having trouble meeting other moms and establishing friendships. Plus I was depressed at times because Joel was out of town a lot on business and the only child-care support we have in town is his mom, who can be quite harsh sometimes in giving me advice and telling me I'm not doing things right."

Laureen was quiet for a moment and then said, "So I guess I was a little vulnerable when I got an email from my old boyfriend, William. We were very close in high school and had a great relationship until we got accepted at colleges that were three thousand miles apart and we went our separate ways."

William had recently divorced his wife and moved into an apartment a few miles from where Joel and Laureen live. According to Laureen, "I don't think William was trying to harm our marriage when he sent that first email. But pretty soon the emails came twice daily and then there were long phone calls where we talked and talked just like in the old days. Within a few weeks, I found myself thinking about him a lot and wondering how to explain all this to Joel."

Joel commented, "When we were in your office a few years ago, we made an agreement to let the other partner know if either one of us started getting obsessed or preoccupied with someone else. I always wondered if we'd have the guts to keep that agreement or if we'd start telling lies and covering up the truth."

Laureen asked, "Are you suggesting I'm not telling you the whole truth?"

Joel replied, "I have no idea. I hope you're not keeping anything secret, but there's no way to be sure, is there?"

Laureen got defensive and said, "Are you saying I'm a liar? That I'm having sex with William?"

Joel looked sad as he commented, "I'll never know for sure, will I?"

Laureen became silent and then said, "I feel damned if I do and damned if I don't. If I were having sex with William, which I'm not, and I told Joel about it, he'd be furious. And if I tell Joel I'm not having sex with William, which is the absolute truth, he's still not sure whether to trust me."

As in most cases where there is a messy flirtation in an otherwise good relationship, Laureen and Joel had hit upon the key issue: the loss of trust and the discomfort that occur with lies, cover-ups, or time delays between the beginning of an outside crush and the time when the couple begins to discuss it.

I suggested to Laureen and Joel, "The sooner you both tell the full truth to each other, the sooner you can begin the gradual and difficult process of rebuilding trust."

For the next several minutes, Joel and Laureen took turns disclosing to each other the various times in their relationship when they'd gotten close to crossing the line with someone. Joel described an incident a few months earlier when he was out of town and an attractive woman approached him at his hotel and said, "I know you're married, but it doesn't matter to me." Joel admitted, "For a second there, I wanted to say, 'Oh, what the heck, I'll never get caught.' But then I thought about the possible confusion that would always be inside my head and the pain that it could cause Laureen and Emma. So I said, 'Thanks for the offer. I'll have to pass.'"

Laureen admitted, "There have been a few times when I was on the phone with William and I thought about inviting him over after Emma had gone to sleep. Then I imagined waking up the next morning and realizing that I would have to spend the rest of my life lying to you and covering up. It made me wonder if we would ever be as close and connected if I did something like that."

After these and other disclosures, Joel commented, "Like I said when we first got married, this is a scary issue in our relationship and we're definitely gonna need to be very careful so we don't wreck the closeness we've built. Especially now that we're raising Emma."

Laureen was looking down at her hands as she said, "I feel horrible that my frequent conversations with William these past few weeks have caused you pain. I had a sense that they were starting to become a replacement for our closeness, and I didn't want that to happen. But I'm also glad we're finally talking again about our relationship and about who we are as vulnerable people. It's been many months since you and I have had a heart-to-heart talk, and longer still since we set aside time to really make love the way we used to. I'm so sorry it took my reaching out to William to force us to remember that you and I are truly best friends and that we need to keep our friendship alive and strong. Even with the stresses of careers and raising a child, I know we can do it."

I've found over the years that when someone in a couple has an affair, a flirtation, or even a lingering curiosity about someone else, it is an important "don't-push-it-under-the-rug" moment for the relationship. It can be a turning point for the partnership, when it either dwindles into mistrust and walled-off feelings, or experiences a profound burst of growth and renewal.

Fortunately for Joel and Laureen, they came in for counseling and began telling the truth *before* the mistrust had grown too severe. During the counseling sessions, we explored their trust concerns and how to rebuild the intense friendship that had always been the foundation of their relationship.

CUTTING OFF CHALLENGING PEOPLE

Sometimes one or both members of a couple say or feel, "I need a break from the person who has been trying to split us apart. I can't let this continue the way it's been." These decisions are quite complicated, especially if the hurtful or insensitive person is an important relative who attends every family gathering; you don't want to lose contact with the rest of your extended family because of this person. Or maybe a co-worker or friend won't stop trying to cause trouble in your relationship, and yet you don't want to sacrifice your job or your friendships because of this one individual. Or perhaps someone from your past has reappeared and stirred things up, yet this person has some good qualities you don't want to miss out on.

While I don't think it's a good idea to make generalizations about when to endure and when to cut off a divisive or trouble-making individual, I do urge each couple to talk this over and to ask themselves three important questions:

1. Is there a way to maintain a strong united front as a couple, even when we occasionally visit, call, or have written correspondence with this friend, co-worker, or relative who has been doing things that could split us apart?

2. Or do we need a break with little or no contact with this person so we can strengthen our own relationship before we deal with this person's difficult behavior again?

3. Or do we need some counseling or coaching on how to stay strong and united before we even try to decide whether to cut off this person?

With regard to the question of whether it's safe to keep talking to someone who has been driving a wedge between you and your partner, I let Joel and Laureen make that decision. Joel commented, "I don't want to be a prick and insist that you can't have a friendship with William. But I'm concerned that he might not understand just how much this marriage means to us and how it's not going to work if he still acts like the handy-dandy replacement friend when I'm out of town."

Laureen replied, "I've thought about this a lot and I have to admit that I did get a sense recently that William might be looking for more than an email and phone friendship. My gut tells me he would love to see if this can lead to something more, and I'm not comfortable with that at all. So I know I'll be sad if I have to let go of my old friend. But I've got to be honest about this. He's way too involved in my life right now, and I do need to focus on rebuilding the daily closeness that you and I deserve to have. I'm willing to go cold turkey and stop the emails and phone calls with William. But I'm going to need you, Joel, to check in with me at least once a day when you're out of town for the kind of playful and enjoyable phone calls we used to have when we were first dating. Who knows, maybe at some future time when William is married again we can all be friends and take our kids to Disneyland. But in the meantime, our marriage has got to come first, and I'm going to tell William directly that that's my number one priority."

Joel put his arms around Laureen and said, "I was worried that this was going to destroy our closeness. But in many ways it's caused me to love you even more. It took guts for you to tell me about this as quickly as you did. And I know it's not going to be easy to let go of a good friend, even if he is a stinkin' home-wrecker."

They both laughed and gave each other a long squeeze. That

session was the beginning of a much-improved relationship be-tween Joel and Laureen. They've called every few months to let me know that they are still keeping their promise to each other to have quality conversations and deep closeness on a daily basis, even when their lives get hectic or one of them is out of town.

Please note: If you or your partner have begun to cross the line into a serious flirtation, affair, or preoccupation with someone else, get help as soon as possible to sort out your feelings and stop the cycle of lies, partial truths, cover-ups, and mistrust. The longer you wait, the harder it will be to repair. But if you get help, there is a good chance that, with honesty and courage, you both can turn a messy situation into a breakthrough for the long-term strength of your relationship.

COMING THROUGH FOR EACH OTHER DURING LIFE'S TOUGH MOMENTS

This chapter addresses a serious issue that shows up in almost every relationship sooner or later: how to stay strong as a couple when one or both of you are going through an especially difficult time. It could be when one of you is physically ill. Or it might be when one of you loses a job, gets passed over for a promotion, or feels trapped in a deteriorating work situation that economic necessity won't let you quit. Or it might be when one of you is emotionally drained and you need your partner's understanding because you are caring for a close relative or friend who is seriously ill or has special needs. Or maybe you or your partner are getting on each other's nerves because one of you is struggling with depression, anxiety, mood swings, or a recurring problem with food, drugs, or alcohol.

Rather than letting life's difficulties tear away at your relationship, you might address the challenge head-on by asking yourself:

* What are some effective ways to help each other and become even stronger partners as a result of this current dilemma?

✳ How might we support each other's personal growth and healing without breathing down each other's necks or becoming critical?

✳ How might we deal with the natural tendency to want to fix each other's situation, or to tune out when one of us brings up the same difficult dilemmas over and over again?

✳ How might we stay healthy and focused when one of us is feeling pessimistic or discouraged?

✳ How might we use the current dilemma to take us to a deeper level of love and mutual understanding, instead of letting it split us apart?

WHY COUPLES CLASH DURING A CRISIS

When counseling good couples who are dealing with painful life situations, I often find that one partner needs a certain kind of support, but the other partner offers something different, leaving the first partner frustrated or upset. You sit down at the end of a stressful day or you call one another on the phone, and, instead of having a supportive conversation, it turns into an argument.

For example, have you experienced any of the following when dealing with a financial problem, a career dilemma, a health issue, or how to care for a family member or friend in crisis?

* Does one of you want to talk at length about a particular problem and the other partner prefers not to talk about it at all?

* Does one of you tend to act on problems quickly, while the other partner tends to go slowly and make careful decisions?

* Does one of you want to get the best advice or assistance that money can buy, while the other partner wants to solve the problem with as little outside help as possible?

* Does one of you tend to be optimistic about what will occur in the situation, while the other partner tends to be pessimistic?

* Does one of you feel resentful that this problem has entered your life and is putting stress on your relationship?

SAYING THE WRONG THING

How the two of you deal with life's toughest moments can make an enormous difference in the long-term success of your partnership. Obviously, if it were easy to be flawless partners during trying times, we wouldn't be discussing this complicated topic. But we might as well be realistic about this—it's not easy to find the right words or actions when you or your partner are upset. That's why many good people say or do things during these moments that make matters worse. As an illustration, let's look at Alana and Jake's case and see if it resembles what you've seen in your own relationship.

"I Was Just Trying to Be Helpful"

When Alana and Jake got married eleven years ago, their lives were running smoothly. They were doing well in their careers, they were physically vibrant, and they had healthy parents.

Since then, Alana has had to deal with the death of her father, who had a fatal heart attack five years ago. She's also had to respond to the many complexities of raising two young children, one of whom has special needs. Alana stopped working outside the home several years ago and has tried with mixed success to work part-time from home.

Jake has wanted to be a supportive partner, but he's also felt discouraged at times, especially because his own career prospects have declined since his company went through a painful series of cutbacks and layoffs. Jake was able to keep his job, but he's working longer hours and has a lot more stress than before.

In the middle of this, Alana's mother was diagnosed with a chronic and debilitating illness. Also in the past year, Jake and Alana found out that their second child, Robert, has severe learning disabilities and social skills deficits that have been causing frequent problems at school, when doing homework, and when playing with other kids. As Jake described it, "Every few months we get another bomb dropped on us from Robert's teachers or counselors, telling us the problem is more serious and harder to resolve than we had imagined."

According to Alana, "When we got married and promised to be there for each other in sickness and health, richer or poorer, I thought our relationship would be strong enough to handle anything. But now I'm worried that the stresses from our financial problems, my mom's illness, our son's struggles in school, and the tension that keeps building up between us is taking the joy out of our marriage."

Jake added, "Almost every other day we have an argument because we've got such different ways of dealing with stuff like this. Alana wants to talk and talk and talk about what it all means and spend a long time analyzing various decisions. But my whole day at work is filled with frustrating problems, so at night I wish I could come home and hear a little good news once in a while."

Alana got upset when she heard Jake asking for "good news." She commented, "That's Jake. When I try to bring him up to speed on what's going on with my mom's illness, with Robert's learning disabilities, or with other important issues, I often sense he is tuning me out. Or he cuts me off by trying to offer a superficial quick fix or some 'Just do this' piece of advice. Sometimes I wonder if he really cares."

Jake snapped back, "Of course I care. But no matter what I do or say, Alana gets upset with me. If I keep my mouth shut and just listen, she'll say, 'Why are you silent? Don't you have anything supportive to offer?' And if I do offer some advice, she also gets upset. Last night I tried to give her a reasonable suggestion about what to do regarding her mother's physician and Alana practically bit my head off."

Alana explained, "I was trying to describe how hard it is to get through to my mother's doctor, and instead of understanding the complexity of what I was saying, Mr. Fix-It blurts out, 'Let's get rid of this doctor and find a new one.'"

Jake replied, "I was just trying to be helpful. You and I both know that your mom's doctor is an arrogant ass and he's driving you crazy because he's so hard to reach."

Alana said, "Yes, but he's my mother's best chance for recovery, and he's the expert on her particular illness. I wasn't asking if we should fire him. I was trying to get some support for how exhausting it can be trying to reach him."

Jake threw up his hands and said, "See what I mean? If I don't say anything, she thinks I don't care. And if I do say something, she doesn't appreciate my suggestions. Lately with all the stress we're under, I just can't win."

WHAT WORKS (AND WHAT DOESN'T) DURING HARD TIMES

Like many couples, Jake and Alana wanted to come through for each other and yet it was extremely difficult to know what to say and do during rough times. So we discussed three things they—and you—could do to reduce the clashes while increasing the closeness and teamwork necessary in times like these.

ASK YOUR PARTNER DIRECTLY WHAT HE OR SHE NEEDS

Jake truly wanted to be helpful, but when he offered quick, decisive advice, he inadvertently brought on Alana's anger or frustration. As Jake admitted during one of our counseling sessions,

"When I see Alana going through a hard time, I feel as though I've got to somehow come up with a solution."

Like many well-intentioned partners, Jake hoped his advice would be viewed as helpful. But even if we're highly intelligent, we can't be expected to *guess* what another person really wants or needs. You can't read your partner's mind. Even well-trained professional therapists and social workers are bound to guess wrong much of the time if they don't ask the person directly what he or she is feeling.

Yet letting go of the habit of giving advice is not easy for most people. I remember many years ago, when I was training to be a psychotherapist, I had a wonderful teacher who told the following story of a grieving client.

One morning he counseled a woman who cried with deep grief about the death of her close friend. That night the therapist was on his way to dinner when he saw the woman again, standing by herself, talking on the phone outside a restaurant, with tears in her eyes and her body shaking. The therapist approached the woman and put his hand softly on her shoulder, offering the consoling words, "I know how you're feeling. It must be very difficult." But the apparently grieving client unexpectedly said, "I'm not crying because I'm sad. The person I'm talking to just told me the funniest story!" She was laughing so hard there were tears in her eyes and her body was shaking.

Being a highly trained professional didn't prevent the experienced therapist from being 100 percent wrong in this case. As a psychotherapist, I know from many awkward moments of my own that even well-trained listeners don't quite understand how people are responding to a particular situation unless we first check it out with the person. Admitting that you don't have all the answers doesn't mean you're stupid or that you don't care; it means you know enough to realize you must include the other person in the conversation and not jump to conclusions.

So I recommend that when you and your partner want to come through for each other during a crisis, find out exactly what your partner needs; don't just blurt out advice or suggestions as though you already know. It's much safer and more reasonable to say to your beloved partner, "I'm with you. What would you like right now to help lighten your load?" Or you may say, "This is important. Let's put our heads together on this to see what we can do to be most effective." Or you may say, "Wow! I never realized what you were going through. What could I do to help?"

Ask if your partner wants advice (or no advice), a comforting touch (or no physical gestures of affection right now), talking (or silence), signs of hope (or an acknowledgment of how frustrating things are right now). Instead of cutting your partner off with premature advice and opinions, it's much more effective to open up the conversation by making sure you take turns brainstorming about what might work and what might not work to improve things.

"This Was the First Time I Felt He Was Completely There for Me"

To help Jake and Alana, we discussed ways that Jake could avoid saying "Just do this" to Alana at the moments when she wasn't looking for advice or quick fixes. Instead, Jake began to try listening to Alana with openness, curiosity, and an honest interest in connecting with her.

Later, Jake came into a counseling session and described how he and Alana had a breakthrough conversation the previous night. "Alana was telling me painful news about her mother having a setback and describing specialized tutoring we might have to get to help Robert with his learning disabilities. In the old days—a few weeks ago—I would have been listening impatiently while trying to be the all-knowing expert by saying something like, 'Oh, we can't afford that' or 'No, let's wait a few months before making any decisions.' But this time I made sure to truly listen and be there 100 percent. To my surprise, something amazing happened. I looked at Alana intensely describing how concerned she was about her mother and Robert. When I stopped trying to be the all-knowing expert and just connected with what she was saying, I felt a lot of respect for Alana and what she's been going through. So I said, 'Alana, one of the reasons I love you is because you're so passionate and so committed to doing the right thing. I want to help you with this. Let's talk about what I could do right now and in the next few weeks and months to make this less of a load on your shoulders.'"

Jake admitted, "It was a little risky to be offering to help her out because I'm way overloaded at work right now. But at that moment I absolutely wanted to lighten her load and be more involved than I've been."

Alana looked relieved as she said, "This was the first time I felt that he was completely there for me in all this. Jake was always quick to give advice or criticize my decisions as though he was my supervisor visiting from the corporate office and I was the lowly employee in the trenches. But this time I really felt like I had a genuine partner and that we were going to find ways to support each other one day at a time through these complex family dilemmas. It felt wonderful."

Jake smiled as he listened to Alana. "You know, it's funny. As a guy, I always thought it was my job to sound in charge or in the know, even on stuff where I don't know diddly-squat. But this time I just took to heart how much Alana is handling on her own now, and I offered to brainstorm with her on ways I might help, even though I've got a lot on my plate already. It was a relief not to have to be the perfect know-it-all for once and to just be a partner. That started a great conversation in which we came up with several realistic ways to help her mom and Robert without either of us getting burned out or overextended."

If you or your partner has fallen into the habit of being an expert in everything, a know-it-all, or the one who gives out quick fixes or advice that the other person doesn't enjoy receiving, try something new. To deeply connect with each other, listen with your whole heart and then ask, "What can we both do to be true partners on this?" These are the magic words that will make your relationship strong during the most stressful of times.

ANNOUNCE THREE SMALL TRIUMPHS EVERY NIGHT

During rough times, couples are bound to experience frustrations and setbacks. But what about the small triumphs—the moments of courage, persistence, creativity, and closeness that need to be re-membered and appreciated?

To unwind and replenish each night, take five or ten minutes with your partner and tell each other a few things that went right that day—even on the toughest of days. These Three Small Triumphs may seem minor: you got a good parking spot close to the doctor's office; or you got through to your HMO after only ten minutes on hold listening to the lousy institutional music instead of the usual twenty minutes; or you found a way to have dignity and be calm when someone was telling you difficult news; or you took a few min-utes to enjoy a beautiful sunset or a favorite old song on the radio.

Or the Three Small Triumphs might be bigger deals. Maybe a work contact finally came through to set up an important inter-view; or you saw a small but undeniable sign of improvement in an ailing loved one's condition and it gave you hope; or you got to spend quality time with someone you care about deeply.

"I Actually Look Forward Now to Coming Home at Night"

In Alana and Jake's case, their nightly five minutes of exchanging Three Small Triumphs made a huge difference in their relationship. As Jake described, "I actually look forward now to coming home at night and knowing that it won't be all bad news. Last night, for instance, Alana told me about how our son Robert had made a small but important step in his ability to focus and stay on-task with his tutor. It might not seem like much to the parent of a child without special needs, but to Alana and me that one small step of progress was as sweet as honey."

191

Alana added, "A few nights ago, Jake came home exhausted from work, and I'd had a very frustrating day because my mother had gotten the runaround again from her doctor, who keeps changing his mind on whether she needs surgery or not. But as soon as Jake and I began our nightly Three Small Triumphs, the mood changed. Jake told me about how pleased he was that he'd talked to an understanding parent of one of Robert's classmates and they'd arranged a play date for this weekend. I felt hopeful and deeply appreciative. Sure, our son Robert has some social difficulties, but if Jake and I keep coaching him and helping him have successful play dates, eventually Robert will have more confidence about making and sustaining friendships."

As you can see, the Three Small Triumphs don't have to be earth-shaking. But if they gratify and inspire you and your partner, they can build a valuable sense of positive strength and teamwork no matter how complicated your dilemmas are. Instead of being split apart by frequent frustrations and setbacks, mention and take to heart the moments of courage, persistence, creativity, or closeness to keep your relationship strong even during trying times.

RECHARGE YOUR BATTERIES SO THAT YOU *CAN* COME THROUGH FOR THOSE YOU LOVE

Many people become so emotionally and physically drained during a financial crisis, a career dilemma, a health problem, or a caregiving ordeal that they become short-tempered or impatient with their loved ones. It's not as if you consciously say to yourself, "Hey,

I've got a good idea—I'm so stressed right now, I will make sure at some point today to take out my frustrations on my beloved partner who is not the cause of the problem." But impatience just slips out at the most unfortunate moments.

In fact, during rough times, most good people try so hard to come through for their kids, parents, friends, clients, or colleagues at work that they simply don't feel as if they have any time or energy left to take care of themselves or their primary relationship. When you're dealing with a crisis that has daily frustrations and tough decisions, you probably aren't getting enough sleep. You might get overwhelmed by too many details and painful choices. Your appetite for food might be more intense than usual, or you might forget to eat (or be too busy to eat a good meal), even when your body is depleted.

Also during a crisis, you might neglect the stretching, exercise, or healthy routines your body and mind need in order to stay clear and productive. As a result, your moods may become volatile or sluggish, causing you to snap at your most cherished loved ones.

Now let's get specific about your current situation: What is required to make sure you get enough rest, exercise, sustenance, and basic self-care so that you *can* come through for the people who are depending on you? I urge you and your partner to take a two-minute inventory each day to ensure that you will be able to respond effectively to your current crisis. Focus on three things:

Replenish your physical self so that you won't snap at your partner. This might mean working out for a half hour, taking a brisk walk to clear your mind and regain your sense of endurance, and eating foods that make you feel healthy and at your best rather than sluggish, short-tempered, or numbed out. Instead of neglecting your physical care, give yourself the nutrition, rest, and exercise that will keep you strong and focused.

Replenish your emotional self so that you won't snap at your partner. Ask a supportive friend, counselor, or loved one to help you sort out, each day or each week, the issues that are weighing heavily on your mind. Or take a few minutes every few days to check in with someone from a support group, or at a resource hotline, who can offer solid advice, or save you time and energy, because he or she has traveled this road before. Sometimes the best way to take care of your emotional self is to set aside five or ten minutes a day to ask yourself, "What do I need right now in order to prevent emotional or psychological overload? Is there help or assistance that I've been unwilling to request, but which might help me now if I admit I'm only human and I can ask for support?"

Replenish your spiritual self so that you won't snap at your partner. Whether you consider yourself a highly spiritual person, a somewhat spiritual person, or not a very spiritual person, make sure you take a few minutes each day to pray or meditate—or to listen to music, look at art, tend a garden, be in nature, or read an inspiring book or quotation—to regain your core strength and your much-needed sense of connectedness.

Prayer, for instance, is not just about asking a higher source to remove all problems. Sometimes the most powerful and effective prayers are the ones that ask for strength, wisdom, or patience to help you find the right words and actions to be of service to those you love. Even if you aren't sure what to say in a prayer or meditation, use these quiet centering moments to open your heart to a mysterious source of creativity and strength. Ask someone from your spiritual or religious tradition for suggestions of ways to ask for strength and endurance during rough times, or come up with your own heartfelt and original words to say to the Soul of the Universe or your own soul: "Help me find the strength to be of service here. Help me see how I may be useful and do what is best."

"I Didn't Grow Up with a Good Feeling about Religion or Prayer"

Alana admitted during one of our counseling sessions, "I didn't grow up with a good feeling about religion or prayer, especially because I saw a lot of hypocrisy and big talkers who said one thing but did another. So it's been years since I really prayed. But lately I've been feeling a desire to ask God, or the creative spirit of the universe, or whatever, to give me strength and courage to deal with all that's going on right now."

As a result of this desire, Alana started her own twice-daily ritual of spending a few minutes talking to what she calls "the mysterious creative Source that I sense deep within my soul." During these silent prayers, she sometimes asks for strength and courage. Sometimes she asks for guidance and clarity of mind. At other times she just asks for patience and an open heart. Alana described how "I'm still not 100 percent a believer, but almost always I come away from these quiet meditations with a renewed sense of energy and hope, as though I'm tapping into a source of strength and wisdom that is beyond words."

Jake said, "My issue is more physical than spiritual. I know from past experience that I definitely need at least fifteen minutes a day of intense physical exercise or I get sluggish, cranky, and short-tempered. When my career was going well and before we had kids, I almost always found time to get some decent exercise four or five days a week. But now with all the pressures at work and the time-consuming issues at home, I sometimes go for weeks or months with very little exercise and lots of junk food."

After we talked about what caused Jake to be sluggish or short-tempered, he began to set aside ten to fifteen minutes per day, five days a week, to take a brisk morning walk or to run in place while watching the morning news. Or he took an invigorating walk during his lunch break or a run with the family dog after work.

Alana reported, "Jake is a lot less stressed and a lot easier to talk to now that he's getting exercise and eating less junk food. He's also looking quite attractive, which is a bonus that I'm enjoying as well."

If your own life right now has a lot of stress, I hope you will consider using some of the techniques above. Difficult family challenges and frustrating work experiences show up during almost every long-term relationship, so please make sure you and your partner respond to these moments with as much wisdom, creativity, and teamwork as possible. Even if your partner doesn't join you in the physical, emotional, or spiritual steps you take to stay healthy and positive each day, be sure to do them anyway, and don't judge your partner for having a different way of coping. The goal is not to compete or argue about whose health regimen is better, but to do whatever you can to stay strong, loving, and supportive of each other during even the most difficult times.

WHAT IF YOU OR YOUR PARTNER IS IN NEED OF CARE?

The previous case of Jake and Alana addressed how to stay close as a couple when the stresses from your ailing parent, troubled child, or fluctuating career are causing tension. But what about when the stress is coming from a mental disorder, a physical condition, a personal limitation, or an addictive behavior that you or your partner have brought to the relationship?

If your partner is struggling with mood swings, hormonal changes, depression, anxiety, panic attacks, sleep problems, or other issues, what works and what doesn't work for helping your loved one deal with these complex challenges?

Or if your partner has an eating disorder, or a problem with alcohol, drugs, gambling, or other addictive behaviors, what is the best way to help without becoming your partner's watchdog or adversary?

Or if your partner has a physical condition that needs treatment but your beloved won't get proper care or follow the practitioner's advice, what should you do to help while still respecting your partner as a grown-up capable of making his or her own decisions?

Or if your partner is floundering in his or her career and needs advice and an improved set of options, how do you offer your help without making your partner feel criticized or belittled?

In many relationships, finding a balance between assisting your mate and not smothering him or her with too much help is crucial if you want your relationship to stay strong and positive during difficult times. For example, here are two final illustrations of couples I counseled in recent years who had to change the way they dealt with each other to ensure that an ailment, disability, work crisis, or addictive behavior didn't tear them apart. See if either couple sounds like you or someone you know:

THE VIGILANT MONITOR
AND THE DEDICATED DRINKER

A creative couple who had been extremely successful in the film business came to my office to talk about the problems they were having with their twenty-two-year-old unemployed son. It quickly became apparent that, in addition to the financial and family issues, there was a lot of tension between the husband and wife because the husband, a film editor named Gene, had a drinking problem that his wife Lucia, an actress, was unable to persuade him to address.

Lucia had tried for years to talk Gene into entering various treatment programs or going to twelve-step meetings, but Gene was completely unwilling. He had been a mostly good husband to Lucia and a caring father much of the time to their three children. Even though his drinking had caused him to lose a couple of good jobs and important work relationships lately, he told Lucia emphatically during their initial counseling session, "I do not have a drinking problem, and I'm not willing to give up one of my few pleasures in life. So don't go there."

Yet according to Lucia, "Every few weeks Gene has one too many glasses of wine or other drinks, and he gets quite moody and verbally obnoxious. Sometimes he insults me or our eldest son in front of other people. Or he'll be sarcastic and somewhat hurtful to one of our dinner guests who might be an important contact for a plum work assignment. I wish I could get Gene to face up to his problem, but he's a very strong-minded person."

At that point, Gene rolled his eyes and said, "I thought we were here to talk about our son."

Lucia replied, "We *are* talking about our son and how your drinking causes you to say things to him that you would never say if you weren't wasted. It's all connected. Like last week when you insulted him at dinner, and then you told that director's wife that her husband is a whore for money."

Gene replied, "Well, he is a whore, and, by the way, I was not drunk when I said it."

"You had five glasses of wine."

"Two," he said.

"Five," she said.

Gene replied, "Bullshit. You make this stuff up."

Lucia explained, "You had one before the guests arrived. One during the appetizers. One with the meal. One with dessert. And one on the balcony where you told her that her husband was a whore for money. Which pissed me off because he was thinking about asking you to edit his next film, but now he's wondering if he wants to have you anywhere near the project."

At that moment, Gene seemed ready to storm out of my office.

He stood up and said, "This happens every time we see a counselor. My den mother here goes into a sermon about how everything boils down to a few glasses of wine. The fact is I do not have a drinking problem. I was never in contention for working on this director's horrible but very commercial film. And I think we're wasting our time here if that's what you want us to be dealing with. We came to talk about how to get our son to move out and get a life."

With most couples where one partner is a dedicated drinker and the other partner is a vigilant monitor of every move the other person makes, this adversarial, me-versus-you contest simply doesn't work. In your own relationship, if you've become the vigilant monitor of someone's addictive or unhealthy behaviors, or the vigilant denier of someone's constant accusations, please note that something has got to change!

"You Treat Me like a Criminal for Having a Couple Glasses of Wine"

To help them, I asked Lucia, "How long have you been monitoring Gene's drinking?"

Lucia smiled and said, "It's been quite a while. Ever since the final year of Jimmy Carter's presidency, I think."

"Has it worked?" I asked.

Lucia thought for a moment and replied, "Apparently not."

"Would you like to try something different?"

Lucia's face lit up. "You bet I would."

So I asked Lucia to say calmly and nonjudgmentally to Gene, "I need your help. Tell me what would work and what wouldn't work if I wanted you to cut back on the drinking so that it doesn't go all the way to sarcasm or hurtful comments, especially to friends who might be able to help us find employment. Teach me what I'm doing wrong that makes you want to go against me and what I can do instead so we can be partners about this. I'll be the student; you be the teacher."

Gene hesitated for a moment and then asked, "Are you serious? Do you really want me to teach you what causes so much friction between us about my drinking?"

Lucia took her husband's hand and said lovingly, "I do want to work together on this. I'm tired of having this issue drive a wedge between us."

As it often does, this calm and nonjudgmental tone of voice began to make a difference and break the pattern of vigilant monitoring/vigilant denial. Gene sat up and said to Lucia, as if they were partners again rather than adversaries, "I have felt so judged by you over the years. So closely monitored and treated like a bad person. The fact is that I do love a glass of fine wine, and I'll even admit that sometimes the wine causes me to say or do things I later regret. But if you treat me like a criminal for having a couple of glasses of wine, I guarantee that I will resist whatever you're saying, even if you're 100 percent accurate. However, if you talk to me like I'm a human being, I'd be willing to make a deal with you before a social event. The deal could be that I'll agree to have only two glasses of wine and I'll make an effort to avoid sarcastic or questionable remarks—as long as you get off my back and stop acting as if I'm this horrible monster. I'm not a monster."

Lucia had tears in her eyes as she said to her husband, "No, you're not a monster, and I will make an effort to talk to you like a human being."

That conversation improved Lucia and Gene's otherwise good relationship. For the first time in many years, they were no longer tense rivals about Gene's drinking. Rather, they were allies who reminded each other gently and playfully before each social event that two glasses of wine was the limit and that sarcastic and questionable remarks were not going to be made.

In addition, over the next several weeks in counseling, Gene became interested in exploring why he was so adamant about drinking and so unwilling to stop. He admitted, "I've always been able to say no to unhealthy foods and drugs that make me less effective in my personal and work relationships, but for some reason I'm quite stubborn about my alcohol."

As with most people who like to drink, Gene was less resistant to change when we started treating him as a decent human being rather than as a guilty party. Those counseling sessions led to Gene facing the fact that alcohol had undermined his parents' marriage, his grandparents' marriage, and two of his siblings' relationships.

As a result, Gene decided to check out a twelve-step program. He described the first meeting as "a room full of losers and complainers." But by the fourth meeting he had changed. He had come to see the meetings as an inspiring and helpful place where he grew tremendously over the next several months. Not only did he stop drinking for the first time, he became close friends with two film industry professionals who helped him line up some excellent jobs, one of which turned into a long-term, lucrative assignment.

While not every person who has a problem with alcohol, drugs, gambling, or other addictive behaviors is as willing as Gene to explore the deeper issues, I hope his case will inspire anyone who has fallen into the role of vigilant monitor or vigilant denier. Certainly we all want to help our loved ones, but, as we saw, Lucia had to lighten up and ask for Gene's help and guidance before they stopped fighting about this complex issue. If you and your partner have spent years battling about an addiction, I hope this case gives you a more loving and less contentious way to help each other.

THE MINIMIZER AND THE REALIST

A final example of what happens in relationships when one person needs care for a serious problem is the case of Henry and Claudia. They had been together for almost a year and were trying to decide whether to get married. Henry was concerned because every so often Claudia suffered from sleep problems and severe anxiety attacks, after which he and Claudia clashed. He wanted to find a way to be on her side when she was going through a rough time, but he found "no matter what I say or do when she's up at night or feeling extremely anxious, it seems to be the wrong thing. I try to reassure her and say encouraging things such as, 'Don't worry. You'll be fine.' Or I'll say, 'It's okay. This will be over soon.' Or I'll suggest, 'Maybe you need to see a different doctor and get different medication for this.'"

Henry added, "For some reason, my attempts to be helpful end up frustrating her or provoking an argument. She says I don't understand what she's going through and that I'm actually making her more anxious. I try not to get frustrated or say, 'What the hell do you want me to say?' But I have to admit it's not easy being up in the middle of the night or trying to comfort an anxious person who gets irritated by each thing I do or say. I think she needs to see a better doctor about this, and, frankly, if she doesn't get better soon, I think I'd be foolish to stay involved with her. Yet I do love her and I don't want to bail out on her, especially since our relationship is so terrific in so many other ways."

Claudia agreed with most of Henry's description of the problem. She said, "It's true that I do get irritated sometimes when Henry says the problem will be over soon, or that I should go to another doctor and take more medications. I've been living with this problem for years, and I've tried all sorts of methods to sleep better and to deal with my anxiety attacks. So I don't appreciate Henry saying, 'Hey, it's no big deal. You'll be fine,' or implying that if I just found the right pill I'd be a completely different person. I realize he's trying to be an unemotional and strong, reassuring friend. But I need him to stop minimizing the problem and help me deal with the reality of what I'm facing."

"What the Hell Do You Want Me to Say?"

Near the end of their counseling session, Henry asked a question that I've heard many concerned partners ask: "Is there some way that I can help her without us getting on each other's nerves?"

That is a crucial question if you or your partner struggle with bouts of depression, mood swings, anxiety, phobias, insecurities, hormonal changes, blood sugar problems (such as diabetes or hypoglycemia), physical ailments, sleep problems, or a chronic disability. You want to help your loved one, but you don't want to be perceived as being critical or impatient, or as pressuring.

What worked for Henry and Claudia works well for many couples. Instead of opposing each other, they became teammates and allies when Henry began asking open-ended questions:

In a calm and patient tone of voice, ask what doesn't feel supportive or helpful when your partner is ailing or upset. Rather than getting irritated or saying, "What the hell do you want me to say?" let go of your ego for a moment and be open to learning what doesn't work and what might work instead.

In Henry and Claudia's case, I urged Henry to say calmly, "Teach me what doesn't feel supportive so I don't keep repeating the mistake." In response, Claudia explained, "When you try to minimize the problem by saying, 'Don't worry, you'll be fine' or 'It's okay, this will be over soon,' you sound impatient or just misinformed about sleep problems and anxiety attacks. Instead of being helpful, those comments make me feel dismissed and rejected by you."

In a nonpressuring and respectful tone of voice, ask your partner what he or she has tried to resolve the problem and whether you may suggest options. Rather than saying or implying that you're going to force your partner to do things your way from now on, loosen up a bit! (Unless partners are severely brain-damaged or self-destructive, they have the right to make their own decisions.) See if you can be more patient and supportive for a while longer. Offer your partner the opportunity to decide when it's time to change course and try new options. Offer to do research and look for alternatives when your partner gives you the go-ahead, but not sooner.

In Claudia's case, when Henry asked respectfully what she'd tried so far and whether it was time for them to explore other treatment options, he learned a great deal about Claudia's intelligence and resourcefulness on this issue. Claudia told him about the various traditional and nontraditional remedies and practitioners she had tried thus far. Then she said, "It would be wonderful if we could research some other methods. I have a few suggestions I want to explore to determine cost, whether my insurance will cover them, and the results the treatments and practitioners have been getting. I'm not promising we'll see results overnight, but I'm happy that you're willing to help and not just assume it's an easy or quick process."

Ask your partner what each of you can do to work together as best friends rather than as competitors or critics. Many couples get into a competition about who's right and who's in charge when dealing with a financial crisis, a career dilemma, a health issue, or a care-giving ordeal. Rather than competing, strengthen your closeness and intimacy by being on the same team and supporting each other's efforts.

"It Felt Like the Two of Us Were on a Mission Together"

In Claudia and Henry's case, they began by discussing how they each felt about various anxiety and sleep treatment strategies that they'd heard about from friends and professionals. Then they divided up tasks, deciding who would call about pricing, insurance, and treatment results. They also asked specialists about new treatments for anxiety and sleep disorders, and about their side effects. At least twice a week they had a fifteen-minute check-in phone call or face-to-face conversation to learn what each had found out.

Claudia explained, "It felt like the two of us were on a mission together. Rather than minimizing the problem or saying the wrong things, Henry had become the most amazing partner I could ever imagine."

Henry added, "I had felt powerless and frustrated for many months watching Claudia suffer and not knowing how to help her. But now we were taking action and we were doing it in sync with each other."

Over the next several months, Claudia and Henry not only saw a dramatic improvement in Claudia's health, they also became closer and more trusting of each other in the process. The health crisis that almost caused them to break up became the turning point that gave them the confidence to make a commitment to be together forever. Henry and Claudia realized that, if they could be excellent teammates and best friends while dealing with frustrating and uncertain sleep problems and anxiety attacks, they could probably handle almost anything.

If you and your partner have been clashing recently because of a complicated or frustrating situation, or you've become distant from each other because you're not sure how to help each other, please take a few weeks to try these realistic, effective ways of strengthening your relationship. I strongly believe that successfully dealing with crises and rough times can be the glue that holds your relationship together, no matter what life presents you. Rather than being torn apart by trying times, the two of you will become more loving and accepting of each other. I wish you strength and courage in whatever challenges you face!

STEP EIGHT

KEEPING YOUR RELATIONSHIP STRONG YEAR AFTER YEAR

In this final chapter, let's look at what you truly believe about relationships. Because if you or your partner don't believe it's possible for a relationship to get better year after year, then guess what? It won't happen.

Let me illustrate what I mean about beliefs. When I was growing up in Detroit, I was warned by several friends in my elementary school that junior high was going to be terrible. One friend said, "They give you a ton of homework and you'll never be able to play again after school." Another friend said, "There are vicious bullies in junior high and you'll get the crap beaten out of you." Yet another friend said, "The bathrooms are totally gross, with no seats on the toilets and no doors on the stalls."

Like most kids, I believed these horrible myths and, as a result, I was reluctant to start junior high. But it turned out the myths were mostly codswallop—a restrained British way of saying "nonsense." Yes, there was homework, but we still were able to play after school most of the time. Yes, there were a few bullies, but one

209

could steer clear of them. True, the bathrooms were not like those at the Ritz, but there were toilet seats and doors on the stalls.

Similarly, a cynical friend, burned-out relative, or sarcastic comedian on television may warn you, "Marriage is a trap. As soon as you say 'I do,' your life is over. No more fun or freedom. You'll lose your identity and your independence." Or someone may say, "Once you have kids, forget about any alone time or passion. You might as well put a fork in it, because you're done." Or someone who's had a disappointing relationship may predict, "Once you've been together for a few years, you'll grow tired of each other. Trust me. Love never lasts."

Like the dreadful warnings about my junior high school, these warnings about long-term relationships are primarily codswallop. But if you are like most people, you may have one or two of these horrible warnings stuck in the back of your brain. This final chapter is designed to expose and outsmart these myths about long-term relationships, so that yours will grow and be more enjoyable year after year.

It's been my experience, in my twenty-four years with my wife, Linda, and with the hundreds of couples that I have counseled, that when people take a few small steps they can overcome these pessimistic predictions about long-term commitments. In the next pages, I will give specific, practical examples of how to make sure your love, your passion, and the needs of your soul get strengthened at every stage of your relationship. Rather than assume that a permanent commitment, or marriage, or kids are the end of your best years, why not try what some creative and intelligent couples have done to make certain that life and love keep getting better with each decade together?

THREE MYTHS AND HOW TO SMASH THEM

If you or your partner have any fears or negative beliefs about a relationship declining over time, please read carefully the following ideas and strategies. You might find that the myths you've been told by "well-meaning" friends and relatives are nonsense, and that you and your partner are capable of achieving more joy and mutual satisfaction than anyone imagined.

MYTH 1: A QUICKIE RENDEZVOUS WITH A NEW PERSON IS MORE SATISFYING THAN WHAT TWO CREATIVE LONG-TIME PARTNERS CAN COOK UP

Newsweek magazine recently tried to sell more copies by running a sexy cover story titled "The New Infidelity." The story implied that long-term love almost always gets boring, and that affairs often spice things up. A great way to sell magazines, but it may not be true for most couples.

In addressing this first myth, I would like you to know that I've talked to hundreds of unfaithful partners, and they've clued me in to something fascinating. These men and women had had one-night stands, quickie affairs, or extended affairs, and they confided that there's some excitement prior to the secret rendezvous, but there's also a lot of emptiness, anxiety, guilt, awkward cover-ups, and obligatory dishonesty when the heavy breathing is over.

People who've had affairs have told me that there's something sadly impersonal and painfully alienating about being physically and emotionally naked right after having sex with someone you don't really love. Most of these clients were surprised by and unprepared for the letdown they felt minutes or hours after an affair—because they had been so caught up in the thrill that comes from the hush-hush secretiveness of trying not to get caught or the mischievousness of doing something forbidden or dangerous.

In the words of one of my counseling clients, "I was on a business trip and I decided to go for it with an attractive woman who had caught my eye and made me feel young and adventurous again. I have to admit I felt rather victorious and powerful for a few seconds while we were going at it—knowing that I'd gotten someone really good-looking to let me do some kinky stuff that I don't think my partner would let me do. It's the kind of thrill you get when you're a teenager and you shoplift without getting caught. You know in your gut it's wrong, but the adrenaline rush from getting away with it is kinda wonderful. But then a few minutes later I was sitting there butt-naked with a person I didn't really know. And I felt a huge wave of discomfort. I had just put my marriage, financial stability, physical health, and future closeness with my kids at risk, for a brief thrill and adrenaline rush. Plus I would have to spend the rest of my days making sure my partner and my kids didn't find out. I voted for Bill Clinton twice during the 1990s, but I truly didn't want to be like him—trying to answer Chelsea's questions again and again about why I was such a horndog and why I had lied so many times to her and her mom.'"

None of us can predict exactly how we will feel or what will happen if we have an affair. Yet nearly all of my clients who've had a one-night stand or an extended affair reported having similar feelings later. When they were sitting with their beloved partner or kids and one of them asked, "So, where were you the other day when I called and you didn't answer?" their whole world felt shattered and fragmented from trying to live two lives. The wonderful adrenaline rush prior to the sex had surprisingly turned into a queasy feeling of dread that they would be found out and screamed at by the people they loved and needed.

Let's compare that feeling of anxious guilt and letdown with the deep sense of connection and oneness that some (but not all) men and women attain when they're fully involved in an exquisite lovemaking session with their lifelong committed partner. I've heard people describe this feeling in the following ways.

"There's nothing quite like making love with the person who is your best friend and who knows your strengths and weaknesses but who accepts you anyway and who's holding you so tightly after such an unguarded round of passion."

"There's a feeling of finally being 'at home'—physically, emotionally, spiritually—that I experience when the two of us have a long, drawn-out lovemaking session that can only happen between two people who thoroughly know each other's likes and dislikes."

"There's a level of soul connection and floating into another world that I've only experienced when I've been deeply in love and we completely know each other's needs and desires. Sure there's a lot of heat and excitement with someone new or with someone who's exotic or different from what I've had in the past. But that sense of newness doesn't compare to the profound surrender and acceptance I feel when my partner and I get hot and heavy after all these years of knowing each other."

If you and your long-time partner haven't had any earth-shattering sex lately (or if you've been holding back from your long-time mate because you're afraid of revealing your full sexual nature), I hope you will take these last few paragraphs to heart. Then set aside an afternoon, evening, or morning with the door locked, or a weekend away from the kids, or maybe even a clumsy make-out session in a parked car like in the old days to rediscover the passionate sparks that the two of you are capable of creating together. Make sure you set aside some times for lovemaking every few weeks, year after year, for as long as you're together.

I'm not going to tell you how to make love or to suggest any specific details—that was covered in Chapter 2. But I do urge you to disprove the myth that passion and heat dwindle with time. When the two of you are rocking and rolling, even after you've been together for five, ten, twenty-five, or forty-five years, I hope you will think about all the people who said you'd grow tired of each other. Those naysayers were wrong about you and your beloved partner!

THE QUEST FOR "HIGH MONOGAMY"

Several years ago journalist George Leonard wrote a controversial book about the difficulties and joys of seeking what he called "high monogamy." He described it as a challenging adventure in which two partners in a long-term relationship seek a spiritual and erotic path together to build a creative, transforming love.

Claiming that high monogamy was a more passionate choice than a one-night stand or ongoing affair, George Leonard wrote, "It's easy to link multiple sexual partners with personal change and monogamy with personal stasis. This can at times be true; but extramarital affairs or the pursuit of recreational sex are far more likely to be associated with the avoidance of change. After superficial erotic novelty has faded and the ego has had its full run (all the life stories told, all the sexual tricks displayed), then the adventure of transformation and a deeper eroticism can begin. But it is precisely at this point that most of us are likely to lose our nerve and leap into another bed, where we can once again tell our stories, display our tricks, do anything rather than see ourselves clearly and start doing something about it. Casual recreational sex is a diet of fast food served in plastic containers. Life's feast is available only to those who are willing and able to engage life on a deeply personal level, giving all, holding back nothing."

According to this perspective of "high monogamy," to fully experience sexuality and love, you must experience it with your remarkable and somewhat imperfect partner. Even if your lovemaking has been less than ecstatic in recent months or years, you may still find a way to experience the joy of finally being "at home" and "at one" with the person whose soul is connected to your soul. I hope you will create some sacred time away from your computer, cell phone, and responsibilities and set up ideal conditions for experiencing a tender and passionate "high monogamy" that will change and grow even as you do.

"We Surprised Ourselves at How Much Love Is Still There"

Here's an example of what I mean by a high monogamy that changes and grows. A couple I counseled had had sexual problems in their late forties and early fifties. Christopher, fifty-two, a human resources executive for a high-tech company, was taking a blood pressure medication that inhibited his blood flow and ability to keep an erection. His long-time partner, Glenn, forty-nine, a marketing executive for a record company, was frustrated because, as he described, "I work in an industry where there are good-looking and willing young candidates for exciting quickies. For years I kept asking myself, 'Why am I saying no to all these opportunities to spice up my sex life?' I do love Christopher and we've built a good life together. But for many years the sexual heat just hasn't been there for either of us."

A few weeks after they entered counseling, I asked them to read and discuss George Leonard's concept of "high monogamy." Then I suggested that they brainstorm answers to the question, "What specifically do we need to do as a couple to put some heat back into our relationship?"

It's a crucial question that I've offered to many couples—gay, lesbian, heterosexual, young, old, well-matched, less-than-well-matched. In most cases it has sparked some wonderful results.

For Christopher and Glenn, this nondefensive and playful conversation about "high monogamy" led them to make a commitment to take three weekends a year to go to their favorite getaway spots for what they playfully referred to as "high monogamy experimental weekends." During these weekends, they planned relaxing and fun activities that both enjoyed thoroughly, along with plenty of time to make love and see what was still possible despite the aging and stress that had crept into their relationship.

After one of these weekends, Christopher and Glenn showed up for an appointment at my office and told me, "You know, we weren't sure exactly what would happen. For years we'd been assuming that we were both too tired, too busy at work, or too stuck in old habits to be hot and exciting lovers again. In fact, we both admitted we were a little nervous about the possibility that this whole weekend experiment might turn out to be another disappointment. But we decided to give it a try, and one morning after we'd been rolling around for a few hours, laughing and having a good time, we surprised ourselves at how much love is still there. Of course the plumbing is never going to be as blindly cooperative as it was when we were twenty years old and capable of getting rock hard just because some young thing walked down the street. But there's something much more meaningful going on now between us. There's a sense of really being 'at home' with each other, of connecting on a deep soul level that no one-night stand and no sweet young thing could ever match."

MYTH 2: YOU HAVE TO GIVE UP YOUR UNIQUENESS TO BE PART OF A COUPLE

You probably know people who seem to suppress important parts of who they are when they are in a committed relationship. For instance, my wife and I know a woman who is brilliant, creative, and fascinating when you talk to her one-on-one. But if she's around her long-time boyfriend, you sense she's holding back, almost disappearing, and showing few or none of her own outstanding qualities. I also know a man who is decisive and self-reliant when he's not in a relationship. But each time he falls in love, he no longer can articulate what he wants or think for himself. It's as though his brain goes on vacation while he lets his partner take over.

As you think about your history in relationships, and your partner's history, does it seem that one or both of you lose your identity or become complacent and unmotivated in a committed relationship? Do you stop growing? Do you stop pursuing the interests, hobbies, and creative passions that nourish your soul? Do you pull away from friends and activities that formerly made you feel alive and involved in the world?

Couples who move their relationship from good to great usually find a way to pursue their separate identities while building a strong identity as a couple. All it takes is for you and your partner to sit down once a month or once a year to ask the following questions:

✳ What activities do each of us love to do, separately or together, that make us feel alive, creative, playful, energetic, and healthy?

✳ What times at night, after work, or on weekends could we do these activities—either on our own or as a couple?

✳ What might we do to ensure a healthy balance of separate interests and combined interests so that our relationship strengthens us as individuals and as a couple?

✳ If we have to give up an enjoyable activity that has become too time-consuming or unhealthy, what other activity might replace it and bring us closer together as a couple (or family)?

You'll notice that these questions are trying to suggest a different reality to dispel the myth that says, "Once you're in a long-term relationship you give up your freedom, your independence, and your fun." Rather than seeing commitment or marriage as a ball and chain, by asking these questions, you and your partner begin to see your relationship as a creative challenge in which you juggle and balance activities that are enjoyable and that nourish your soul.

"I Don't Understand His Passion for Cars, But I Love the Joy It Brings Him"

Alicia and Cory are a couple who found a healthy balance between his individual interests, her individual interests, and their shared passions. They'd been together for three years when they came in for counseling because they weren't sure whether to get married.

Alicia explained, "We are so completely different in some ways. I love to spend a lot of time with my friends and my sister and her kids. Cory can't stand sitting around and listening to my friends talk. He's polite and respectful with my sister and her kids, but he'd much rather be watching car racing or fixing up his own car that he races at a track near where we live. I like to read novels and he hates to read. I like to watch cooking and home-design shows, which he finds extremely boring."

Cory added, "I worry because we're so different from each other and that in a few years Alicia will ask me to give up my interest in cars and racing. That would be a big mistake because, when I'm involved in preparing for a race, or even in watching a race, I escape from all the worries of my career and I feel completely alive and free."

When I asked them what they have in common and what passions they share, Cory and Alicia gave me a blank stare. But then Cory commented, "It's funny. We got fixed up by a friend who loves the same kind of music we love. So when we go to a concert or we put a CD on and listen to it, we always flash back to how great it felt the first year when we used to go hear a lot of music together. But lately we've been too busy to set aside any time for music, concerts, or even CD evenings at home."

Alicia added, "We also both love to go exploring in nature. Cory's a little more adventurous than I am with his mountain bike and rock climbing. But sometimes he's willing to go on a beautiful hike that is more at my cautious level, and we bring along a picnic in our backpacks and have a great time. Unfortunately, each weekend lately has been filled up with my sister's kids and with Cory's car racing. It's been six months or longer since we went exploring in nature."

Like many couples, Alicia and Cory had an important decision to make. Did they want to go along with the myth that a committed relationship means giving up what you love, or drifting apart, or just doing things as a twosome? Or was there some other creative way to combine Cory's passions, Alicia's passions, and their common interests into a balanced schedule that could be more satisfying for both of them?

We sat down and literally drew up a series of weekly and monthly calendars and filled in three types of activities: things that Alicia loved to do, things that Cory loved to do, and things that they loved to do together. All of these would be included in each week's flow of activities.

Once Cory and Alicia saw with their own eyes that it was possible to combine all of these diverse activities into a well-thought-out calendar (that respected them as individuals and supported them as a couple), the question of marriage became a lot less frightening. I added, "The trick is to make sure that, after you are married, you redesign this calendar every few months. Your interests might change. Your life might get more complicated. But if you have frequent brainstorming sessions in which you ask yourselves, 'How do we find the right balance between what you love, what I love, and what we love together?' then the relationship will remain strong and vibrant."

Five years later, I ran into Alicia and Cory at a supermarket and

I asked them how it was going. Cory said with a smile on his face, "We got married a few years ago, and I found out that it's not a trap if we don't let it become a trap. Alicia still has her two nights a week with her close friends and two weekends a month with her sister's kids. As for me, I'm still passionate about car racing and involved with some great racing teams. Plus, as a couple, we've been on some terrific nature trips, and every week we have at least one night where we walk on the shore while catching up on our busy lives."

Alicia added, "What's interesting is that I still don't understand Cory's passion for cars, but I love the joy it brings him. When he's preparing for a race or he's watching an event on television, I can see he's fully alive. I feel lucky to have a well-balanced marriage where we both do the things we love as individuals and we also have great times together as a couple. I always thought you had to give a lot up in order to be married, but now I realize that, if you honestly plan and work it out together, you can make your marriage as satisfying as you want it to be."

MYTH 3: HAVING KIDS IS THE END OF YOUR FREEDOM AND PEACE

I always knew I wanted to raise children at some point. But before my wife, Linda, and I became parents, I remember hearing from one couple after another:

"We used to have great sex . . . until we had kids."

"We used to have great vacations . . . until we had kids."

"We used to have lots of time to talk and be best friends . . . until we had kids."

"We used to have time to unwind and relax each weekend . . . until we had kids."

"We used to think we could handle it all . . . until we had kids."

As a result of hearing these comments repeatedly, I was somewhat concerned that having a child would be the end of life as we knew it during our childless years. At the same time, I was intrigued and impressed by a few of the couples I saw in counseling (and a few remarkable couples in my circle of friends and relatives) who seemed to love and guide their children, but who also kept their relationship and their individual passions alive after becoming parents.

How do they do it? How do some couples make time for all the crucial areas of their lives—family closeness, work, creativity, sensuality, spirituality, personal growth, volunteer involvements, relaxation, and exploration? Here are a few action steps that may help shatter the myth that your adult self will be neglected when you have kids.

Take an hour or two a day of uninterrupted time. I've found that the couples that tend to be happiest are the ones that give each partner one or two hours a day off-the-clock, free, and unpressured. For example, Aaron and Beth had wanted for years to become parents. But they soon found that raising children was far more complicated and exhausting than they had imagined.

When Aaron and Beth came in for counseling, Beth was extremely frustrated because, as she described, "I love my kids, but I get burned out from being up night after night with one kid or the other, plus getting up and making breakfast each morning, plus trying to calm them down and get them to fall asleep each night. When I'm reading that fifth bedtime story and my four-year-old is still awake, I feel my nerve endings screaming for a break."

Aaron sat silently while Beth expressed her frustrations. Then she turned to him and asked, "Do you think it's fair that I'm doing most of the child care, even though we promised to be equal partners in this?"

Aaron got defensive and said, "Hey, it's not easy for me to be up at night with the kids when I've got so much pressure at work right now. If I miss a night's sleep, there are huge consequences."

Beth looked upset as she replied, "Well, it's not easy for me either—spending all day taking care of them and then being on call at night as well."

She looked away from Aaron and admitted, "For me, this issue of who gets up in the middle of the night is not just about logistics or sleep. For me, it's a deeper concern about who we are as a couple, and this concern is stirring up resentment inside me and causing distance between us. I always thought that whatever came up in our relationship, we'd find a way to deal with it fairly and as equal partners. But now I'm realizing that if something like middle-of-the-night child care might inconvenience Aaron or if it's a little bit harder than he anticipated, the fairness and the equality we talked about when we first got married is just not his top priority any longer."

Aaron thought for a moment and then replied. "I'm sorry if

this is hard for you. But this is who I am. I'm very career-focused right now and I can't afford to do anything that might put my job in jeopardy."

Like many couples, Beth and Aaron were struggling over whether they could trust each other to keep growing and improving as individuals and as a couple.

Fortunately, something happened before their next counseling session. Beth was called out of town for a few days to help her ailing father, and Aaron was completely in charge of the kids during her absence.

At their next counseling session, Aaron offered, "I never appreciated how hard it is to be on call twenty-four hours a day until last weekend when Beth was out of town. I'd helped out previously, but I always knew I could hand a crying child over to Beth if it got too difficult. This time, after two long days and nights of being 'on duty,' I felt like a starting pitcher who had thrown too many pitches and had lost his good stuff, yet had to carry on because there was no well-rested relief pitcher coming in from the bullpen to take over. I'd had hour after hour of being at my kids' beck and call. Then when I thought I was finally going to get a break at 9:00 P.M., our four-year-old began bouncing off the walls from being too tired to stay up but too wired to fall asleep. That was the moment I realized just how much Beth deserves more help so she doesn't burn out."

As Aaron, Beth, and hundreds of other couples have taught me, even people who adore their kids need an hour or two a day where they aren't responding to the demands of children. In order to have enough energy to be a good parent and to feel good about your life in general, you need a little relief sometimes. Will you and your partner support each other and come up with solutions that work for both of you, or will you stop growing and stop looking for mutually satisfying solutions?

For the remainder of their session, Beth and Aaron exchanged creative ideas about how to help each other so that parenting would be enjoyable rather than exhausting. After several back-and-forth conversations, they began to develop a balanced and equitable system for backing each other up in raising the kids. As a result of their brainstorming sessions during the second and third counseling appointments in my office, Aaron and Beth codesigned a mutually satisfying weekly system. If one of the kids was sick, anxious, or unable to sleep, Aaron would pitch in on three or four of those nights, and Beth would be the on-call person the other nights that week. To make sure Aaron could still function well at his job, he would not be asked to do two sleep-compromised nights in a row. If he did have to be up in the middle of the night with one of the kids, he knew the next night he'd be "off duty" and could catch up on his sleep.

At the same time, they would take turns making breakfast. Beth would be the breakfast wake-up person three or four days a week, and on the mornings Aaron was the breakfast wake-up person, Beth could sleep late, exercise, return phone calls, or pursue her creative projects.

On weekends, each of them would enjoy at least two hours alone with no responsibilities. As Aaron explained, "Beth and I need some quiet time to read or make phone calls or get some exercise without having to deal with the kids fighting or asking for things. So we began to plan each weekend to include family time together, separate times with each child individually, and a few hours each day where one parent was on duty while the other parent got to take a break. It's made Beth and me far less stressed and far more pleasant to be around because we get to enjoy great moments of being a family as well as important moments of being our own private selves."

If you and your partner are raising children, please make sure you set aside time each week or month to design an equitable schedule that works for both of you. Raising children is a huge commitment, and our children need involved, loving parents. That's why it's crucial for you and your partner to set aside small amounts of escape time each day—to be "off-duty" and to back each other up with quality relief and support.

The better you are at scheduling your "time off," the better job you will do as a competent, patient, and effective parent. Instead of being at the end of your rope much of the time, you will be calm and clear with your family. Instead of snapping at your spouse or kids the first time they provoke you, you will be able to take a deep breath and say to your loved ones, "Hey, let's not have a cow about this. Let's calmly work this out."

Take alternate days on family trips to get some time for yourselves. Several years ago my wife and I developed a method for changing the family trip from an ordeal to a huge and energizing success for each member of the family. We call it the Everybody Gets Their Own Day method. Here's how it works.

227

When we visit relatives out of town, or when we go on vacation to a place where we will be sightseeing or in nature, we take turns letting each family member select the day's activities. We also take turns being on duty or off duty as parents. On the first day in a new city we usually do a family activity together, and my wife and I enjoy some interesting sites with our son, Steven.

Then, on the second day, I usually take Steven on an adventure he picks, while Linda has the day off so she can follow her own rhythms and go to an art museum or nature site that she wants to experience quietly without interruptions. On the third day, Linda takes Steven on a fun adventure she gets to pick, while I get a day on my own to exercise, read books, or find a quiet and relaxing place to be alone and rest.

On the fourth day, we arrange for a family member or a trusted child-care professional to be with our son while Linda and I have a romantic escape day that we design as a couple. (We usually find certified and safe child care by contacting the nicest hotel in town and asking their concierge for a recommendation. Even if we're not staying there, the concierge is almost always polite and helps us find a qualified and bonded child-care person whose hourly rate is reasonable.) This method of honoring your relationship while on vacation with your kids may turn a stressful family trip into a relaxing one. Our son has enjoyed spending time with creative, wonderful individuals in each of the cities we've traveled to as a family.

An illustration of how this teamwork approach may help you balance family time and adult time is a trip my wife and I took with Steven to visit relatives and do some sightseeing in Florida. Normally a two-week trip with our beloved but hyperactive, impulsive son might be exhausting, but we utilized the taking-turns method described above. I enjoy being with my son, but I know that sometimes he needs a break from being with us, and we need a break from being on duty nonstop as his parents.

To make the vacation enjoyable for all of us, we spent the first day together as a family in historic Saint Augustine and went on a tour of Ponce de Leon's Fountain of Youth, the oldest jail in North America, and other sites that we took turns selecting. On the second day, I went with Steven to ghost sites in the old city and a deserted British fort, sites he had selected. Meanwhile, Linda had some quiet time on her own looking at art, swimming in the hotel pool, and taking a much-deserved nap.

On the third day, Linda went with Steven to an alligator farm they chose together, while I had some quiet time alone for reading, catching up on emails, writing, and walking by the ocean. On the fourth day, Steven went miniature golfing and to some historic sites (with a certified and trained child-care person who was recommended by the concierge at the nice hotel we called), while Linda and I got dressed up and had a relaxing candlelit dinner and romantic walk in the quaint old town. Because we took turns asking for what we most needed, we made the vacation a huge success with a large number of positive memories.

If you and your partner have felt exhausted or drained by family trips or by overtired kids who argued about what to do each day, I urge you to try the taking-turns method. It's much more fun to be with your child when you know that you will have some quiet time on your own at some point during the trip, as well as some romantic time as a couple. Rather than arriving home tired and in need of a vacation after the family trip, you probably will feel fulfilled after discovering that life as a parent can include great moments with your family, great moments on your own, and great moments with your one-and-only partner.

Look at your children as a way to learn more each day about patience, humility, commitment, integrity, and love. Some people view their kids as "one more mouth to feed," "one more bill to pay," "one more burden to handle," or "one more unpredictable thing that you can't really control." Or, as a friend of mine said recently, "You don't know about feeling impotent until you try to get a teenager to clean up his or her room."

But there's another way to view parenthood that may bring a tremendous amount of wisdom and fulfillment to your daily life as a couple. Being a parent is one way to learn some of life's most important teachings. It's almost as if I didn't know how to be a complete adult until I had a child to teach me certain lessons.

You may notice each week that your children are helping you learn more about persistence, strength, integrity, and commitment. Let's say your kid comes home from school and describes an upsetting incident. You realize that you are being asked to summon up all your listening skills, social skills, activism skills, and philosophical and spiritual principles to design an appropriate response that will help your kid deal with the incident. Your response may become an important growth moment in each of your lives.

You may find that there's nothing more humbling and heart-warming than the moments you are being of service to an infant, toddler, preteen, or teen who needs your patience, guidance, and steadfast calmness during the ups and downs of daily living. I remember two inspiring stories that were told to me by close friends who have challenging kids.

One friend, whom I will call Patricia, was completely exhausted from a stressful day at work. She was carpooling her son and daughter to after-school activities, and was trying to get them to stop arguing and have some dinner at a buffet restaurant. All of a sudden the argument between her son and daughter got worse, and one of them knocked over the trays carrying their dinners. It was a huge mess, and Patricia was on the verge of screaming some hurtful words that would probably have been remembered by her kids and played back word-for-word in five years in a therapist's office.

But instead of losing it in the restaurant, Patricia said to herself, "Take a breath. Don't go off on your kids. You don't have to be perfect. Just be the solid and reasonable parent you never had when you were growing up. Set limits lovingly. And don't freak out!"

Within a few seconds, Patricia had taken a deep breath and put herself back in charge of the situation. Without getting nasty or ugly, she helped her children cool down and work out their differences. Eventually the three of them were able to eat a relaxing meal together.

As Patricia later told me, "My kids are definitely helping me learn how to become a stronger person. Nothing else in my life has taught me as many lessons about what really matters in the big picture. Before becoming a parent, I never knew just how much I could dig down deep inside to find inner strength that I barely knew was there or that I could be strong and loving no matter how my kids test my patience. It's made me a lot more patient and accepting of my spouse's imperfections as well. I think that one of the reasons our marriage keeps improving is that our kids are forcing us to grow constantly and never settle for what we experienced in our own families when we were growing up."

The other inspiring story about how our kids teach us patience, humility, and integrity was told to me by Dave, the devoted father of an intense teenage girl named Ali.

According to Dave, "I had read in various philosophical and spiritual books about the concept of humility, but I never really understood what humility meant until I agreed to be the responsible adult tagging along to the extremely loud and overcrowded concert that Ali and three of her friends just *had* to attend.

"Talk about chipping away at one's sense of self-importance. I can assure you that no one at the concert knew or cared that I've studied and worked my whole life to become a respected professional in my field. For three hours I was basically a human coatrack, holding the fashionable backpacks and discarded jackets for Ali and her friends while they ran to the mosh pit near the front of the stage and watched the concert with thousands of other screaming teens. They clearly didn't want anyone there to know I existed or that I was related to them."

Then Dave smiled and said, "But thank goodness for humility, because I was glad to be there. It gave me a chance to make sure they were safe and weren't taking drugs or getting hit on by creepy older guys. It also gave me a chance to remember how arrogant and impressionable I was at that age, when I believed my favorite musicians were gods and that my parents didn't know a thing. I thought my daughter was going to continue to treat me like a human coatrack, but to my surprise on the way home—*after* we had dropped off her friends—Ali turned to me and admitted for the first time in months that I'm an okay dad. It was great to hear."

If you have ever been in a situation where you were being of service to one of your kids, you probably realize that spontaneous thank-yous of appreciation are not spoken too often. So please don't hold your breath waiting for a "Dad, you rock!" to pop out of your child's mouth. You and your spouse or partner might wait years for your kids to stop thinking you're a total drag when you set limits lovingly or try to help them learn responsibility and compassion.

If you have kids, I urge you and your romantic partner to say to each other at least once a week (or once a day) that you appreciate all that you both do as parents. Each moment of helping, guiding, or simply being a human coatrack for your child is a holy moment. You are doing the most important and underappreciated job on the planet. If you and your partner take a few moments each day to acknowledge how important your efforts are for your kids, you will not only stay strong as parents, you will add strength and warmth to your relationship.

NOW THAT YOU'RE AWAKE—STAY THAT WAY!

This final chapter has offered numerous examples of why a lifelong commitment and family responsibilities are not the end of your best years but the beginning of a fascinating adventure that can be transforming and fulfilling. Being in a growing relationship, and having your ego challenged daily by loved ones who know you better than anyone, is essential to becoming your best self.

I have attempted in each chapter to increase the fairness, mutual respect, teamwork, and mutual satisfaction that you and your partner bring to each day of living together. I know it's not easy to build a great and long-lasting relationship, but I hope you will try many of the techniques in this book to increase the likelihood that it will happen for you and the one you love.

Improving your relationship and keeping it strong each passing year is one of the least selfish acts you will undertake. May your strengthened relationship be a blessing and a source of healing for the two of you as partners and for your kids, extended family, and community. Our society desperately needs healthy couples who can make it through the stresses of modern living. We live in a time when relationships are falling apart. I urge you to become an exception and to find ways to deepen your love and expand your teamwork so that at the end of your life you can look into each other's eyes and say, "We did it! We defied the odds, and we built something exquisite that was stronger than all the forces that can pull loved ones apart. We had the strength and the persistence to love fully and be loved fully."

In each chapter of this book, you and your partner were given specific ways to become more successful at the delicate and profound adventure called love. I hope that if you hit any additional rough patches in your relationship, you will look back at the eight steps again. The two of you might need reminders of how to find the balance between being too flexible and not flexible enough. Or how to put the enjoyment back in your sexual relationship. Or creative ways to improve the teamwork in dealing with chores, kids, or errands. Or a quick review of how to cool down from a fight and make sure both sides get heard and respected. Or guidance on how to stay united when frustrating situations or difficult people try to split you apart.

Every so often there may be stresses and miscommunications that threaten to send you back to the place you were when you realized it was time to wake up and put new life in your relationship. If that happens, please don't panic. You now have the proven tools and specific methods for keeping your love strong forever. I wish you all the best and I am confident that your life will be more joyful because of the caring, companionship, and shared visions that you and your partner will be able to achieve.

ACKNOWLEDGMENTS

Numerous people were creative, patient, and helpful while teaching me what works and what doesn't work for improving a relationship. First of all, I want to thank all of the couples, individuals, and families who attended my workshops or showed up for counseling so that we could learn together how to make things better.

Next, there have been many teachers, experts, writers, researchers, and mentors whose guidance helped me develop the techniques and methods found in this book. They include John Gottman, Julie Gottman, Margaret Paul, Jordan Paul, Ron Taffel, Pepper Schwartz, Sondra Ray, Lonnie Barbach, Bernie Zilbergeld, Adelaide Bry, Harold Bloomfield, Janet Ruckert, Lynne Jacobs, Gary Yontef, Harville Hendrix, Janis Abraham Spring, Andrew Christensen, Pat Love, Walter Brackleman, Michelle Weiner-Davis, Terry Real, Gay Hendricks, Kathlyn Hendricks, Barbara Ehrenreich, Michael Gurian, Gayle Kimball, James Michael, Sean Austin, and Rowland Shepard.

In addition, I want to thank the following friends and colleagues who taught me valuable insights about how to build a healthy and fulfilling relationship: Peter Reiss, Carol Reiss, Teri Bernstein, Helene Pine, Marie Kaufman, Marc Sirinsky, Catherine Coulson, Ted Falcon, Ruth Neuwald Falcon, Laura Geller, Miriam Raviv, Sandra Kaler, Paul Silver, Sonny Stokes, Catherine Mahlin,

Andrea Bayer, Jayne Danska, Evone Lespier, Glen Poling, Lucky Altman, Cheryl Sindell, and Patricia Amrhein.

This book has been guided and supported by some wonderful professionals, including my brilliant and extremely honest agent, Andrew Stuart; my insightful, caring, and wise editors at Rodale, Chris Potash and Stephanie Tade; and many other great individuals at Rodale, including Cathy Gruhn, Amy Rhodes, Jessica Roth, Mary Lengle, Donna Gould, Dana Bacher, Leslie Schneider, Kelly Schmidt, and Tom Mulderick. Special thanks to Nora Flaherty at Holtzbrinck.

Finally, I want to thank my family members Martin Felder, Ena Felder, Janice Ruff, Craig Ruff, Erica Ruff, Andi Bittker, Ruthe Wagner, Ron Wagner, Nellie Kolb, Bill Schorin, June Schorin, Jeff Schorin, Ruth Wilstein, Mary Ellen Bayer, and Helen Rothenberg Felder for all their love and support, and especially my wife Linda Schorin and our son Steven for teaching me daily about love, commitment, and persistence. I thank God for letting me know such genuine and decent people.

NOTES AND SOURCES

Step 1, page 9

Carrie Fisher described the relationship power struggle as "both of us wanted to be the flower and neither of us wanted to be the gardener who nurtures the flower." This quote was given at a talk she gave for *Postcards from the Edge* in Los Angeles in 1987 and also appears in "Rappin' with Penny and Carrie: The Fastest Gums in the West" by Todd Gold, Special Edition, *People* magazine, Spring 1991, vol. 35, pp. 94–96, and in "Troubled Waters" by Suelain Moy, *Entertainment Weekly*, August 13, 1993, p. 84.

Step 1, page 9

Numerous research studies show that one of the clearest early indications that a good relationship is starting to go downhill is when one partner repeatedly feels he or she is giving in too often and not being respected or taken seriously in response. These studies are summarized in *The Seven Principles of Making Marriage Work* by John Gottman and Nan Silver, New York: Crown, 1999, and in *Reconcilable Differences* by Andrew Christensen and Neil Jacobson, New York: Guilford Press, 2000.

Step 1, page 15

The character Lenny is from *Of Mice and Men* by John Steinbeck, New York: Penguin Books Classics, 1992.

Step 1, page 26

The character who learns about the tactic of "making the partner think it's his idea and then he'll say yes" is from *My Big Fat Greek Wedding*, written by Nia Vardalos, directed by Joel Zwick, IFC Films, 2002.

Step 2, page 51

The character who says "Please baby, please baby, please baby please!" is from *She's Gotta Have It*, written and directed by Spike Lee, Island Pictures, 1986.

Step 2, page 52

The workshop where deep breathing, patience, and Tantric sexuality were discussed is "The Sexual Rebirth Workshop," taught by Margo Woods, March 1979, San Diego, California.

Step 2, page 56

The self-pleasuring techniques are described in *For Yourself* by Lonnie Barbach, New York: Anchor Books, 1976.

Step 2, page 58

Recent research showing that many men and some women become habitually attracted to porn can be found in several places: on the Web sites for Sex Addicts Anonymous; on the iVillage Web site's interview with psychotherapist Dr. Brenda Shoshanna; in the research studies of Dr. Victor Cline, available from his Morality in Media Web site; and in the 1998 San Jose Marital and Sexuality

Center study reported on MSNBC.com that interviewed 9,265 individuals and estimated 17 percent were vulnerable to porn addictions that interfere with their daily lives.

Step 2, page 72

The scene with Meg Ryan's character is from *When Harry Met Sally*, written by Nora Ephron, directed by Rob Reiner, Castle Rock Films/Nelson Entertainment, 1989.

Step 2, page 77

Various research studies, each stating that well over 50 percent of women prefer oral sex, can be found in *Sexual Behavior in the Human Female* by Alfred C. Kinsey, Bloomington: Indiana University Press, 1953; "The Sexual Response Cycle of the Human Female" by William Masters and Virginia Johnson, in *Sex Research New Developments*, New York: Holt, 1965, pp. 90–112; *The Hite Report: A Nationwide Study on Female Sexuality* by Shere Hite, New York, Macmillan, 1976; and "Female Orgasm: The Role of the Pubo-coccygeus Muscle," *Journal of Clinical Psychiatry*, vol. 40: pp. 34–39, 1979.

Step 3, page 88

In recent years there has been a controversy in which John Gottman's research at the University of Washington has critiqued the "active listening" style ("I hear what you're saying") that couples counselors used to teach most couples. Instead, Gottman and others have demonstrated through numerous studies that the active listening style is too hard to follow for most couples, and what's more important is that certain types of listening are still a killer to most relationships, especially a harsh, negative start-up to the conversation, or too much criticism, contempt, defensiveness, or dismissive body language. Gottman claims to be able to predict with 96 percent accuracy which couples will get divorced based on these listening factors.

Step 3, page 104

Research by Bluma Zeigarnik that shows the brain is focused on problems and incompletions, rather than what's going well, is summarized in *Seven Prayers That Can Change Your Life* by Leonard Felder, Kansas City, MO: Andrews McMeel, 2001, pp. 22–23; *The International Encyclopedia of the Social Sciences*, vol. 5, New York: Macmillan, 1968, p. 407; and the original *Das Behalten erledigter und underledigter Handlungen, Untersuchungen zur Handlungs und Affektspsychologie*, No. 3, *Psychologische forschung* 9, 1927, pp. 1–85.

Step 5, page 133

The character played by Renée Zellweger is from *Jerry Maguire*, written and directed by Cameron Crowe, Gracie Films/TriStar, 1996.

Step 5, page 134

The psychological phenomenon of feeling you are 100 percent right and not finding it easy to shift to the possibility that another point of view might also be right is called "cognitive dissonance" and is described by Leon Festinger in *Extending Psychological Frontiers: Selected Writings of Leon Festinger*, by Stanley Schachter and Michael Garzzaniga, New York: Russell Sage, 1989.

Step 6, page 157

"My earlier book" refers to *When Difficult Relatives Happen to Good People* by Leonard Felder, Emmaus, PA: Rodale, 2003.

Step 6, page 167

For more on how to deal with flirtations and infidelities, see *After the Affair* by Janis Abrahms Spring, New York: Harper Collins, 1996.

Step 7, page 198

To get a list of twelve-step meetings in your area for helping people overcome problems related to alcohol, drugs, overeating, gambling, debt, intense emotions, or other habits, look in your local phone book under Alcoholics Anonymous, Narcotics Anonymous, Cocaine Anonymous, Gamblers Anonymous, Debtors Anonymous, Emotions Anonymous, etc. Or if you are a friend or family member who is dealing with the ups and downs of a loved one's problem, look up Al-Anon or Narconon in the phone book to find local meetings.

Step 8, page 211

The cover story on "The New Infidelity" by Lorraine Ali and Lisa Miller appeared in *Newsweek* magazine, July 12, 2004.

Step 8, page 215

The discussion of "high monogamy" is from *The End of Sex* (later retitled *Adventures in Monogamy*) by George Leonard, Los Angeles: Tarcher, 1983, pp. 155–156.

ABOUT THE AUTHOR

Leonard Felder, Ph.D., is a licensed psychologist in West Los Angeles whose nine books have sold over 1 million copies and have been translated into fourteen languages. In addition to *Wake Up or Break Up*, his titles include *When Difficult Relatives Happen to Good People*, *The Ten Challenges*, *Seven Prayers That Can Change Your Life*, *Making Peace with Your Parents*, *When a Loved One Is Ill*, and *Making Peace with Yourself*.

A widely requested speaker, he has appeared on more than two hundred radio and television programs, including *Oprah*, *The Today Show*, CNN, *A.M. Canada*, ABC Talk-Radio, and National Public Radio.

Originally from Detroit, Michigan, Dr. Felder is a Phi Beta Kappa and High Honors graduate of Kenyon College in Ohio. He is active in several volunteer organizations and has won the Distinguished Merit Citation of the National Conference of Christians and Jews for developing programs to overcome racism, sexism, homophobia, and religious prejudice.

Leonard and his wife, Linda Schorin, have been together since 1980 and they are the parents of a 12-year-old son, Steven.

RODALE

LIVE YOUR WHOLE LIFE™

Every day our
brands connect
with and inspire
millions of people
to live a life of the
mind, body, spirit
— a whole life.